USBORNE GUIDE TO THE

SUPERNATURAL WORLD

Eric Maple
Eliot Humberstone
Lynn Myring
Designed by
Iain Ashman

Contents

The material in this book is also published
as three separate titles in the Supernatural Guides series:
*Vampires, Werewolves & Demons; Haunted Houses, Ghosts & Spectres;
Mysterious Powers and Strange Forces*

1

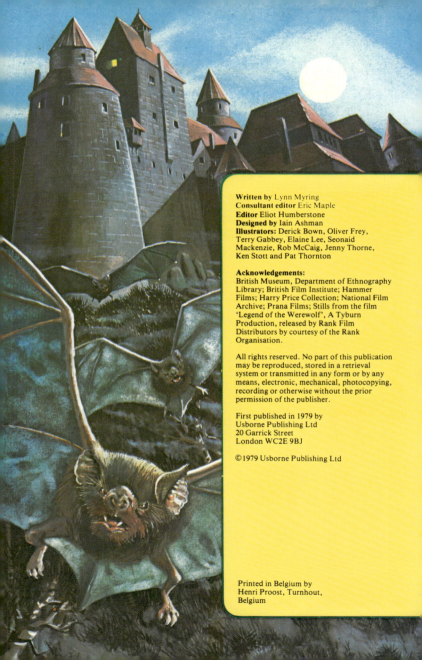

Written by Lynn Myring
Consultant editor Eric Maple
Editor Eliot Humberstone
Designed by Iain Ashman
Illustrators: Derick Bown, Oliver Frey,
Terry Gabbey, Elaine Lee, Seonaid
Mackenzie, Rob McCaig, Jenny Thorne,
Ken Stott and Pat Thornton

Acknowledgements:
British Museum, Department of Ethnography
Library; British Film Institute; Hammer
Films; Harry Price Collection; National Film
Archive; Prana Films; Stills from the film
'Legend of the Werewolf', A Tyburn
Production, released by Rank Film
Distributors by courtesy of the Rank
Organisation.

First published in 1979 by
Usborne Publishing Ltd
20 Garrick Street
London WC2E 9BJ

©1979 Usborne Publishing Ltd

Printed in Belgium by
Henri Proost, Turnhout,
Belgium

Part 1
VAMPIRES
WEREWOLVES & DEMONS

Introduction

Throughout the world, stories have been told of horrible, bloodsucking creatures called vampires, and of werewolves and other werebeasts, which were people who could change into animal shapes and do evil deeds. For centuries, many people lived in fear of these evil beings. They even invented special techniques to destroy them and protect themselves.

This part contains stories based on first-hand reports by people who genuinely believed they had been attacked by vampires and werewolves. It shows how these creatures are thought to have looked and acted, and gives some of the possible reasons for these haunting and incredible legends.

Contents

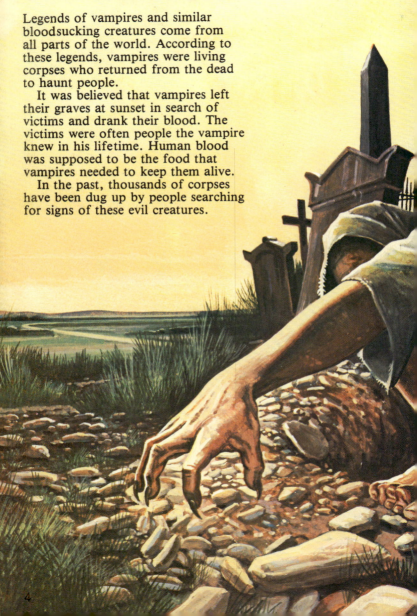

What is a Vampire?

Legends of vampires and similar bloodsucking creatures come from all parts of the world. According to these legends, vampires were living corpses who returned from the dead to haunt people.

It was believed that vampires left their graves at sunset in search of victims and drank their blood. The victims were often people the vampire knew in his lifetime. Human blood was supposed to be the food that vampires needed to keep them alive.

In the past, thousands of corpses have been dug up by people searching for signs of these evil creatures.

The undead

Vampires were often thought to be violent criminals or people who had died suddenly. Anyone who committed suicide, or who was the victim of a vampire's attack, was also thought to become a vampire.

Often such a person had not had a proper burial and it was believed that the spirit, unable to go to heaven or hell, remained active in the corpse. This is why vampires were known as 'the undead'.

The most terrifying stories of vampires come from Eastern Europe—where Polish vampires, for instance, were said to float in blood-filled coffins. Their Russian relatives were supposed to take the blood from a victim's heart. Most vampires, however, preferred to attack at the neck, puncturing the skin with razor-sharp fangs until the blood flowed.

The blood preserved the vampire's body so it did not rot in the grave like an ordinary corpse. If a vampire's coffin was dug up the body looked as if it was asleep, rather than dead.

Vampires worked at night, under cover of darkness, often creeping into a bedroom while an innocent victim lay sleeping. If the victim was not completely drained of blood in an attack, the vampire would return the following evening.

5

The ways of the vampire

People in countries as far apart as Hungary and China have believed in the existence of bloodsucking vampires. Not all vampires behaved in the same way.

Many were thought to be able to fly or change their shape. Most were accused of attacking animals as well as humans, for blood to drink.

In some areas the vampire was a bodyless ghost. In others there were arguments about what animated the vampire corpse; an evil spirit or the return of its original soul, unable to rest in death.

▲European gypsies believed the vampire left his bones behind when he rose from the grave. He roamed around at night, waking sleepers, breaking things and making a terrible noise. He also harmed cattle by riding them at breakneck speed over the fields.

From beyond the grave

Not all vampires had to dig through the earth to reach their victims. Some were not bound by the ordinary laws of nature. They were said to escape from their graves by taking on a misty shape. In this form they could seep through the coffin and six feet of earth that covered them and become solid again above ground.

As they made no disturbance to the soil, the only sign of a vampire's resting place was the hole through which the misty body flowed. Locked doors were no problem either. Unless the wise occupant had rubbed garlic around the frame, the vampire would simply assume his misty form and slide underneath it.

▲ Almost all legends tell of vampires drinking blood from the living. Some were also thought to attack fresh corpses. They not only drank the blood but sometimes even ate the flesh of a dead person. They were also blamed for spreading foul diseases.

▲ Some vampires were supposed to be invisible and very spiteful, breaking anything they could get their hands on and spitting blood all over the place. These vampires beat their victims black and blue, flinging them about in an attempt to get at their blood.

7

Varieties of vampire

Europe was terrorized for many centuries by vampire beliefs. The Ancient Greeks feared human-like demons that drank blood from the living. The Norse people of Scandinavia believed the dead were alive in their graves, but had become evil and violent.

Vampires were not reported in Britain after 1300, but they haunted the rest of Europe for much longer. As recently as 1863 there was a vampire epidemic in Bulgaria. It did not end until a witch discovered and destroyed the evil spirit.

Monsters of the night

▲The Russian vampire (shown left), known as a 'vieszcy', gnawed his own hands and feet while in the grave but at midnight he escaped to attack cattle, seek blood and ring church bells.

The Bulgarian vampire had two forms. For the first 40 days he learned how to be evil and had a filmy body which gave off bright sparks in the dark. After this the vampire rose from the grave in his old body, but he now had only one nostril and a long sharp tongue.

In Transylvania, now part of central Romania, there was a vampire called the 'murony'. It could change from a human into a cat, dog, toad or any blood-sucking insect. This sort of disguise made it very easy for the murony to attack his victims, as they would not be suspicious of animals. When discovered in human form in the grave, the murony could be recognized by its long sharp nails and the fact that blood dripped from its eyes, ears, nose and mouth.

Many central Europeans believed that a soul could leave its body and enter into an animal without any ill effect, even before death. Some people thought it was dangerous to go to sleep thirsty as the soul would then go out to look for a drink. The soul often took the shape of a mouse or flying insect.

▲These three figures are types of German vampire. On the left is a 'neuntoter', blamed for spreading plague as it had such an unpleasant, smelly body and was covered in sores. In the middle is a 'dracul', a vampire corpse that was brought to life by a demon. The vampire on the right is a 'nachzehrer' which had very strange habits. It sat in its tomb holding the thumb of one hand tightly in the other, always kept its left eye open, and made loud grunting noises while it devoured its shroud.

Preventing vampires

People terrified of vampires found many ways of protecting themselves. Ointments and charms to ward off the undead were sometimes sold, but wild roses, garlic, fire and crosses were said to give the best protection.

Although it was possible to kill vampires it was far more important to try and prevent a suspect corpse becoming one and leaving its grave in the first place. A vampire's bite turned its victims into new vampires when they died. They hypnotized people while feeding on their blood so the victim remembered nothing of an attack and a vampire could return several times to drink blood, undiscovered and unfeared.

Victims of a vampire's bite were not the only corpses said to join the undead. Anyone who had a violent or mysterious death or had been very evil when alive, was thought likely to return as a bloodsucker.

Anyone at all unusual in appearance or behaviour was supposed to become a vampire. In Greece, where red hair and blue eyes are uncommon, they were said to be signs of the undead. Great care was taken with such suspects when they died and corpses were always watched and never left in the dark.

Guarding the coffin

The picture below shows a night-time scene following a death. The precautions taken against vampires illustrated here were used in many parts of Europe in the 15th and 16th centuries.

Sun and moon light were once seen as strong sources of life-giving energy, which might be able to reactivate a corpse. Curtains are still shut today if a death occurs, perhaps because of this old belief.

Being creatures of the night, the undead were terrified of lights and fires. Torches were lit outside the house and plenty of candles and a large roaring fire protected the people inside.

Vampires hated garlic and anyone who did not like it was thought rather suspicious. It was hung around rooms, rubbed onto doors, window frames and even farm animals to ward off vampires.

Animals were a great danger to the unburied corpse. If one jumped over the coffin, the body inside was sure to become one of the bloodsucking undead. Even the animal might turn into a vampire at death.

Mirrors were thought to reflect the soul and were taken down or turned to face the wall near a corpse. This was to prevent the soul becoming trapped in the mirror and returning later to animate the body.

Burying a vampire

Some burial customs still observed today may have started as ways of keeping the undead in the grave.

Flowers were first put in or on coffins in the belief that they would bind the spirit and prevent it coming back to haunt the living. Wild roses were used when dealing with vampires.

Graves were dug deep, so that plenty of earth held down the corpse if it tried to escape. Graves were also marked out, as walking over a corpse was said to turn it into a vampire.

▲People who committed suicide were thought to become vampires. They were pinned in the coffin with a stake and buried at the crossroads. This was done to confuse the vampire, so he would not find his way home to attack family and friends.

▲Heavy stones were placed over the vampire's grave to prevent it climbing out. Where piles of rocks were used in place of a single big boulder, travellers were supposed to add a stone or two if they did not want to be chased home by the vampire.

▲Skeletons have been discovered riveted to the graves like the one shown above, or with their leg-bones broken to stop the corpse walking. Sometimes red ochre was painted on in the hope that this blood-coloured clay would satisfy the need for real blood.

At the grave-side

If people suspected they were haunted by a vampire they searched the graveyard for the blood-drinking beast.

Once it was found, there were many ways of killing a vampire. These varied from place to place, but a common method was to drive a stake into its heart with a single blow. Sometimes red-hot nails replaced the stake and they were often hammered into the head as well. Ripping a vampire's heart from its body to boil in oil or beheading it with a gravedigger's spade made quite certain that it could not rise again from the grave.

The picture below shows some of the precautions taken when a vampire was found, or someone thought likely to turn into one was buried. The body was staked face down into the coffin so it could not climb out. Crosses of willow wood were put under the arms and holy water sprinkled in the grave to repel evil demons which were thought to re-animate some corpses. The mouth was filled with garlic so it could not bite anything.

Tiny seeds were scattered in the grave and churchyard as vampires were said to count every one. This would take so long that dawn would break and the vampire would have to return to the grave without having time to find a victim.

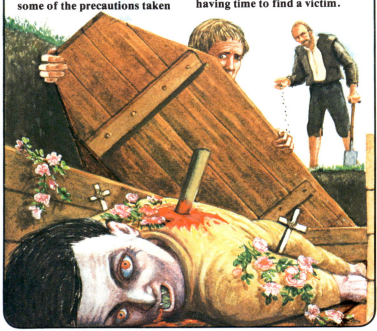

Plagues and vampires

Thousands of people were killed by the outbreaks of plague which swept Europe during the Middle Ages. It spread very quickly, with such terrible effects that normal life often ground to a halt. Buildings fell into disrepair, farming was neglected and people fled from infected areas if they could afford to. There was no cure for plague.

There were more reports of vampires during times of plague, and vampires were often blamed for spreading this terrible disease.

Plague was thought to hang in the air like a mist, so people tried to disturb it with loud noises, bells and music. The church bells that tolled for the dead were also believed to frighten away vampires.

Vampires were also scared off by large bonfires, known as need-fires. Animals were driven through the smoke and embers, and the ashes were scattered on the fields to protect them from the evil, plague-spreading vampires.

Plague victims had to be buried quickly because of the danger of infection. They were collected by the gravedigger and dumped into open pits outside the village. Infected houses had a cross marked on the door.

Disease was thought to be God's punishment for people's sins. The church offered protection from plague with special rituals and prayers. Processions went round villages sprinkling holy water and carrying crosses and pictures of the saints. These were thought to get rid of vampires and other demons.

Starving animals attacked and ate bodies flung in the burial pits. The blood-covered remains were blamed on vampires. One kind of plague caused a deep sleep that was easily mistaken for death, so some people were accidentally buried alive. These were the 'corpses' that did not rot and tried to escape the grave.

Herbs were burned to cover the stench of rotting bodies with sweet smells. The smoke was said to ward off vampires and destroy the plague in the air.

People believed the vampire spread plague and created new vampires with each attack, so the only way to end an epidemic of plague, or vampires, was by finding and destroying the vampire corpses. Many suspect bodies were staked, beheaded and burned to ashes in places hit by plague.

15

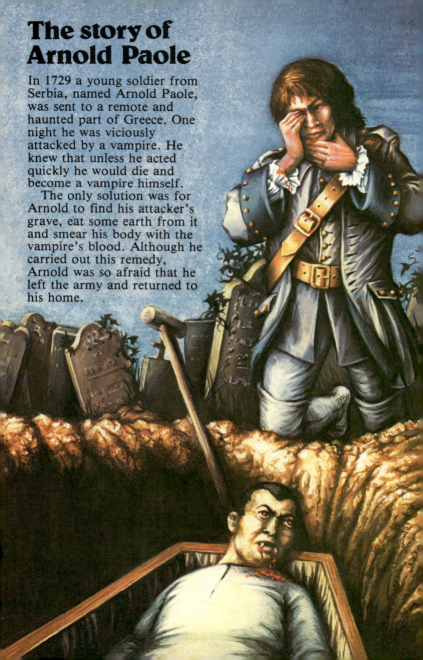

The story of Arnold Paole

In 1729 a young soldier from Serbia, named Arnold Paole, was sent to a remote and haunted part of Greece. One night he was viciously attacked by a vampire. He knew that unless he acted quickly he would die and become a vampire himself.

The only solution was for Arnold to find his attacker's grave, eat some earth from it and smear his body with the vampire's blood. Although he carried out this remedy, Arnold was so afraid that he left the army and returned to his home.

1. Arnold settled on his small farm in the village of Meduegna, and seemed to be quite unharmed. However, during the harvest he fell from a hay cart and died soon after. He was buried in the local churchyard, but did not rest there in peace.

2. Within a month Arnold was seen wandering the village at night. People who saw his spirit became very ill and four died within a few days. Panic spread and it was decided Arnold's body must be dug up and checked for any signs of vampirism.

3. This gruesome task was carried out one grey winter morning about ten weeks after Arnold's funeral. The gravedigger dug up the coffin, watched by officials from the capital city and army doctors as well as the local dignitaries.

4. When the coffin was opened, what it revealed made everyone certain they were dealing with a vampire. Arnold had moved to one side of the coffin. His hair and nails had grown and his mouth was red with fresh blood. He looked like a living man.

5. Arnold's corpse had to be dealt with in one of the traditional ways for ending vampirism before his soul could rest quietly. The villagers scattered garlic over Arnold's body and said prayers for his spirit. A stake of whitethorn wood was driven into his heart with one blow. Warm crimson blood gushed from the wound, as if Arnold were still alive— although he had been buried over two months. The corpse writhed in agony and let out a dreadful yell.

6. The four victims of Arnold's night time attacks were dug up in case they had become vampires too. The reports of this epidemic of the undead in Meduegna do not mention the condition of these corpses.

However, it seems they were vampires, as they were dealt with in the same way as Arnold had been: stabbed by whitethorn stakes and beheaded with a spade.

Finally all the vampires were thrown onto a roaring bonfire and burned in its fierce flames.

7. Fire was supposed to be the ultimate weapon for destroying vampires. A pile of smouldering ashes is impossibe to revive. Once deprived of an earthly home the vampire's soul was forced to go to the spirit world.

Although all the vampires had been staked, burned and reburied, within six years a new epidemic broke out in the village. Once again people were taken ill and became pale and weak as if from loss of blood.

They died suddenly just like Arnold's victims.

8. The villagers now knew how to deal with the danger, and another party of investigators arrived from Belgrade. They examined every suspicious grave and found many corpses in a vampiric state. These included children, and even small babies, as well as adults. All were full of fresh blood, so they were dealt with in the usual way. The ashes were thrown into a river to carry them away. People suspected the new epidemic had been caused by eating meat from animals once attacked by Arnold Paole.

Ghostly vampires

The most usual kind of vampire was a corpse brought back to life by a demon or by the original spirit, unable to rest in death. Sometimes the vampire was merely a spirit or ghost and did not need a body in its hunt for blood. This sort of vampire occurred most frequently where people worshipped and feared the spirits of dead ancestors.

Witches and sorcerers were thought to send out their souls to steal blood and do evil even before they died. Their bodies fell into a deep trance and did not recover until their souls returned.

▲The 'ekimmu' of Ancient Assyria were the ghosts of people who had not been properly buried. They became very hungry and thirsty and as no offerings had been made to them, they sucked the blood of the living. Their appearance meant certain death.

▲These hideous witches were the 'civateteo' from Mexico. Said to be the ghosts of women who died in childbirth, they stole babies to eat in revenge. They were thought to gather at crossroads so people left them offerings to save their children.

▲Australian aborigines saw blood as the strength of life and fed it to the sick. They also made blood-offerings to the spirits of dead relatives and cut themselves when in mourning. If the blood was not given freely the ghost grew angry and stole it.

20

An African elephant spirit

Many African tribes also made offerings of blood to the ghosts and spirits of their ancestors. Some spirits seemed to be happy with animal blood, but if they were not honoured by blood sacrifice they would return and spread illness and death among living relatives.

Ghosts became more unpleasant and dangerous the longer they were dead and it was important not to offend them. Sometimes the spirit returned as a ferocious man-eating animal.

The picture below shows the spirit with the trunk of an elephant said to haunt the Fan people of central Africa. Ghosts were sometimes said to cause death by eating the victim's heart or liver

Eastern vampires

There are many Chinese vampire legends, similar to those found in Europe. Some were said to be demons, but others were thought to be animated by the original souls, called the P'o. These were believed to remain on earth for a short time after death when they could turn their bodies into vampires.

▶ Any corpse that did not rot was considered to have become a vampire. But even skeletons or just a skull could be possessed by demons and brought back to life. Chinese vampires often learned to fly and sometimes ate other corpses for food.

▼ Japanese vampires, like this giant double-tailed cat, were very evil spirits that could assume the shapes of hideous animals. They even disguised themselves by assuming the likeness of their human victim after hiding the corpse.

Liu, a vampire's victim

A teacher named Liu had just returned home after tending his ancestors' graves some distance away.

His wife went to wake him next morning, but, to her horror, found his corpse lying on the bed. It was completely drained of blood. A vampire had stolen the head to finish his feast of blood.

Liu's wife ran screaming from the house but was promptly arrested and put in jail.

On a nearby hillside a man gathering wood noticed a coffin lying neglected near an open grave.

People who came to investigate removed the lid of the coffin. Inside was the hideous vampire. It was covered in shaggy green hair and had sharp fangs and claws but a face like that of a living man. Liu's missing head was clutched tightly in the arms of the vampire.

23

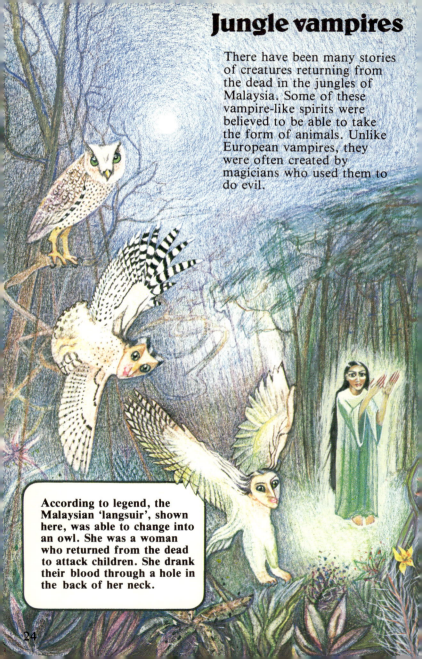

Jungle vampires

There have been many stories of creatures returning from the dead in the jungles of Malaysia. Some of these vampire-like spirits were believed to be able to take the form of animals. Unlike European vampires, they were often created by magicians who used them to do evil.

According to legend, the Malaysian 'langsuir', shown here, was able to change into an owl. She was a woman who returned from the dead to attack children. She drank their blood through a hole in the back of her neck.

Demonic Vampires

▲ This tiny vampire, called the 'polong', was no bigger than the top joint of a man's little finger. It attacked people with the help of a demonic house cricket known as the 'pelesit'. This burrowed into the victim's body making an entrance for the polong to get in. They caused a terrible madness which often made the patient rave about cats.

The polong and pelesit were usually created by magic. The polong was made from the blood of a murdered man, kept in a bottle for a week while spells were said over it. The pelesit was made from the tongue of a dead baby. Once created these demons had to be fed on blood every day.

One of the most unpleasant demons of the Malasian jungles, shown below, was known as a 'bajang'. It was believed to take the form either of a polecat or a lizard.

Some bajangs were made out of the soul of a freshly buried child that had died at birth. A magician would visit the grave in the middle of the night and persuade the spirit to come out of the corpse by chanting magical spells.

Bajangs were suspected of attacking people when someone had a mysterious illness. The main symptoms of an attack by a bajang were fainting and convulsions. Like many vampirical beliefs, the supposed activities of a bajang served to explain any illness that people did not understand.

The way to destroy a bajang was to find its creator and destroy him. If the person suspected of controlling a bajang drowned in a river, the bajang, in the shape of a lizard, was said to escape through the nose of the drowning person.

Why believe in vampires?

Do vampires really exist? Up until the nineteenth century thousands of people all over the world thought that they did.

Now, we can explain the facts that started the vampire myth in more sensible ways.

Today, few people believe corpses can rise from their graves to attack the living and drink blood. This is not because we are more intelligent, but simply that life is so very different now.

In the past people were far more superstitious, but their belief in vampires was based on a great deal of evidence which seemed to have no other explanation.

Mysterious things seemed to happen in graveyards. Strange, dark figures were seen wandering among the tombstones at night, and frightening noises were heard coming from graves.

When people investigated, they sometimes found graves open and empty. Even more horrific were the coffins which contained twisted, blood-stained corpses, their shrouds all tattered and dirty. Others revealed life-like bodies which had remained quite unrotted in the grave. People thought they had discovered blood sucking vampires. It is more likely that these were the remains of people buried alive.

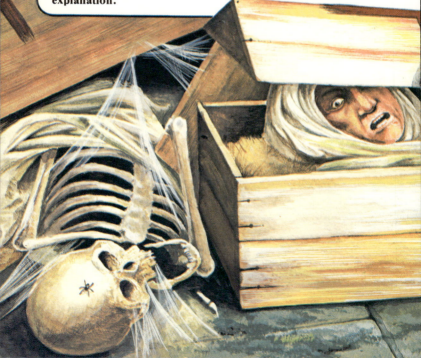

The picture on this page is based on a painting called 'Buried Alive', by the 19th century Belgian artist, Antoine Wiertz.

Premature burial has been common in the past and is not unknown even today. Sometimes it is quite difficult to be certain that a person is dead. One doctor suggested that the only way to be sure is to wait for the body to decompose.

A rare illness called catalepsy puts victims into a death-like trance of suspended animation, which can last for days or even weeks. The patient appears to be dead but if buried in this condition might wake in the coffin; only to die slowly of suffocation or starvation. Many must have tried to claw a way out of the grave and bitten at their own flesh in desperate hunger. No wonder these blood-filled coffins and horrific gory corpses started rumours of vampires.

The bodies that disappeared from graves had not climbed out in search of warm living blood to drink. They were more probably stolen by the 'Resurrection men'. These body snatchers stole fresh corpses and skeletons from their graves and sold them to doctors who wanted them for medical research.

27

The vampire in fiction

Stories about vampires have been written for thousands of years. Even Ancient Greek and Roman authors wrote about the dead who returned from the grave to drink blood.

The vampire theme proved so popular in eighteenth century Germany that many poets wrote ballads about ghostly vampires. These inspired later writers, such as Edgar Allan Poe and Bram Stoker, to produce horror stories that are still successful today.

Most recent vampire fiction has been written for films or for the theatre.

▲Lord Ruthven, an early stage vampire of the 1820s, was a character from a story 'The Vampyre'. This tale was begun by the English poet Lord Byron, but was completed by his friend Dr Polidori, who modelled the vampire on Byron.

Count Dracula

This classic tale of vampire horror was a success when it first appeared in 1897 and has not been out of print since. Dracula's author, Bram Stoker, had the idea for this story after a terrible nightmare. He researched the vampire legends of medieval Europe in the British Museum and decided to use Transylvania as a setting.

In the novel, the evil Count Dracula lives in a dark crumbling Transylvanian castle with a group of female vampires. However, he has bought an old abbey in England and plans to move there in order to spread vampirism throughout the land.

▲A young English lawyer, named Johnathan Harker, visits Dracula to arrange the transport for this move. Harker soon realizes that Dracula is a vampire. He is made a prisoner and the Count leaves for England.

Varney the Vampire

First published in 1847, this huge book was so popular that it was soon reprinted in 220 episodes, each selling for one penny. Its author, Thomas Prest, also wrote several other cheap 'penny dreadful' serials.

Varney the Vampire, subtitled 'The Feast of Blood', is set in England in the 1730s. It tells the tale of the Bannesworth family, plagued by a vampire named Sir Francis Varney.

Varney is basically a good person—but he was driven to evil by bad luck. He drinks the blood of Flora Bannesworth and kidnaps her lover. After many adventures Varney kills himself by jumping into the volcanic crater of Mount Vesuvius.

▼Dracula kills the entire crew of the ship to drink their blood and once in England he attacks Lucy Westenra. She dies and becomes a vampire, terrorizing London until a Dutch expert on vampires, Dr Van Helsing, drives a stake into her heart.

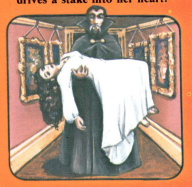

▲Harker escapes and helps Van Helsing search for Dracula, who has attacked Harker's wife. They chase the Count back to Transylvania, and plunge a knife deep into his vampire heart.

Introducing werewolves

Werewolves were evil, savage people with the power to turn themselves into wolves. Living on a diet of human flesh and blood, they roamed at night searching for lonely travellers to attack and eat.

Some were said to become creatures that were half man half wolf, others to change into wolves completely. It was believed that a werewolf could turn his skin inside out to hide the fur when in human form. Many people accused of being werewolves had their bodies ripped open in the hunt for this wolf fur.

It was, however, possible to recognize the werewolf in his human shape. Werewolves were supposed to be very hairy, with straight bushy eyebrows that met in the middle and small pointed ears. Often the third finger of each hand was as long as the second, and hair grew in the palms of the hands.

Traditionally the werewolf returned to human shape once it had been injured and could be traced by the trail of blood it left behind. The most effective way to kill a werewolf was with a bullet or knife made from the silver of a melted crucifix. The corpse had to be burned rather than buried, as it was believed a werewolf would rise from its grave as a vampire.

Legends tell of men turned into werewolves by a curse or dreadful accident. Doomed to become wolves each night or with every full moon, they welcomed death as a release from this fate.

People all over the world have believed in werewolves, and a rare mental illness called lycanthropy was also recognized in ancient times. This disease makes patients think that they can turn into wolves, although they do not. However, they usually behave like werewolves, murdering people and eating the flesh of their victims.

31

Becoming a werewolf

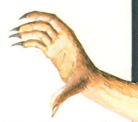

Some people were believed to turn into wolves during a full moon against their will. However, some bad people actually wanted to become ferocious werewolves and they used magic to bring about the transformation.

A Russian legend said it was necessary to jump over a fallen tree in the forest, stab it with a small copper knife and chant a spell to become a wolf. Drinking water that collected in a wolf's paw print or eating the brains of an animal killed by wolves were sure ways of changing into a wolf.

In many parts of Europe, legends grew up about exactly what sort of magic acts were supposed to be able to turn somebody into a wolf.

A typical magical werewolf ritual is shown below.

▲ A would-be-werewolf made his transforming ointment at midnight when the moon was full. He put wolfsbane, opium, foxgloves, bat blood and fat of a murdered child into a pot and boiled them.

▲ When this nasty mixture was ready the werewolf took off his clothes and rubbed the ointment into his skin. He put on his pelt of wolf fur, chanting spells and incantations, asking the wolf spirit to turn him into a wolf.

After the ritual of
the ointment was
carried out, the
man was expected
to turn into a
supernatural wolf-
like creature with a
lust for human
blood and flesh.

Once he had
managed the evil
transformation, the
man changed into
a werewolf every
night, and back into
a man each
morning. The
spell was broken
by death or if the
werewolf was
stabbed three times
in his forehead.

European werewolves

Stories of werewolves sprang up in most countries where real wolves were a danger to the population. There have been very few wolves in Britain since the Middle Ages, and the last wild wolf was hunted down some time in the 18th century.

The discovery of a real, but rare, strange disease called 'lycanthropy' increased the terror of the legend of the werewolf. Anyone suffering from lycanthropy believed himself to be a werewolf.

This form of insanity sometimes lead to people trying to act as if they were real wolves. In France especially, there were many trials of people accused of lycanthropy.

▼These fearsome Norse warriors, known as the Berserkers, added a great deal to the werewolf legends of Europe. They wore wild animal skins and grew long hair and beards to give themselves a frightening appearance.

Isolated villagers attacked by these murderous invaders probably thought they were half animal. The Berserkers were said to be able to turn into ferocious bears and wolves during battles.

A Norse saga tells how a wizard put a spell on two wolf skins, so whoever wore them became wolves for ten days. These skins were discovered by two warriors, Sigmund and Sinjoth, who took shelter in a forest cabin. Unaware of the curse, they stole the hides from the men asleep there.

Once put on, the skins would not come off. Sigmund and Sinjoth howled and attacked the sleeping men and even bit each other. They broke the spell by burning the skins when they fell off ten days later.

According to an Irish story, a priest who was lost in some woods found a wolf sitting by a fire. It spoke in a human voice and asked the priest to give the last sacraments to his wife, who was dying. The wolf explained that his family had been cursed, so one man and one woman had to spend seven years as wolves. If they were alive after this time they could become human again.

The priest did not believe the story until the she-wolf ripped open her wolf skin to reveal her true shape as a woman.

France has many legends about werewolves. One medieval story tells of a hunter who fought off a huge wolf that attacked him in the forest. He slashed off one of its forepaws, but the beast escaped and the hunter put the paw in his bag. Returning home, he was amazed to find it was changing into a woman's hand.

He recognized a ring on one finger as one he had given to his wife. Rushing upstairs, he found her lying in bed, bleeding from many sword cuts with a stump where her hand was missing.

A French wolf-boy

In 1604 Jean Grenier, a 13 year-old French boy, was accused of being a werewolf. He claimed a mysterious man, the Lord of the Forest, had given him a magic wolf skin and ointment that turned him into a wolf. For three years he ran about the forest as a man-eating werewolf.

1. Jean Grenier admitted eating more than 50 children. He had a craving for raw human flesh and found little girls most delicious. When very hungry he would even attack a crowd of people.

Passing through a village one day he found a baby sleeping in an empty house. Jean could not resist such a tasty meal and as no-one was in sight dragged the child from its cradle.

He carried it off to the woods and shared the bloody remains with a real wolf that joined him later.

2. Another child had more luck. He was playing at the edge of the wood when Jean attacked suddenly. The werewolf leaped out of a dense thicket and, hurling himself at the boy knocked him to the ground and snapped at his throat. The boy would have been torn apart if his cries had not been heard by his uncle, who was nearby.

The boy's uncle rushed up shouting at Jean 'I'll get you now'. Eventually he managed to beat off the werewolf with his heavy stick.

3. One afternoon three girls out tending their sheep found Jean lurking in some sand dunes. His strange appearance frightened them very much. He was thin and dirty, dressed only in rags. His thick hair was matted, his teeth and nails like those of an animal rather than a boy and his eyes were wild and ferocious. The oldest girl asked why his skin was so dark. Jean replied it was because he was a werewolf and if the sun were to set he would eat them. The three girls immediately ran away in terror.

4. Jean Grenier was proud of his adventures as a werewolf and bragged about them to a girl named Marguerite Poirier. She told her parents that Jean scared her but they thought little of her stories until she was attacked herself. Marguerite said that a wild beast, like a wolf but with red fur and a stumpy tail, had leaped upon her. It ripped her clothes with its fangs, but she beat if off with her staff. The beast was so frightening that Marguerite ran home as fast as possible.

5. The attack on Marguerite led to Jean Grenier's arrest and trial before the parliament of Bordeaux. Jean claimed that he was a werewolf and confessed that he had murdered and eaten people. His accounts of the attacks were the same as those of the witnesses and victims. Marguerite was the only one who thought he had been in the form of a wolf but there was no doubt that he was a murderous cannibal. Two doctors were called in and said Jean was suffering from lycanthropy.

6. The judge thought Jean was so dull and idiotic that any child half his age had more sense. He discounted rumours of witchcraft and shape-changing and sentenced Jean to spend the rest of his life in a monastery at Bordeaux.

After being taken there Jean still behaved like an animal, running on all fours and eating any raw meat he could find. The judge visited Jean seven years later and found him less wild— but still claiming to have been a werewolf.

39

Werewolves in America

North America has many legends of people who could turn into animals, but not all of them were werewolves.

The ancient Indian stories often tell of marriages between people and animals. Usually the animal could remove its skin and was a man or woman underneath.

Some tribes believed they were descended from such a marriage and so were related to a particular animal. Some warriors were even said to send their spirits out in the body of an animal and would die if it was harmed.

▲Canadian Indians who pretended to believe in Christianity were said to become werewolves. According to legend, they turned their skins inside out at night to change into wolves and then went off into the woods to attack true Christians.

◄Canada was colonized by many French people, who brought with them their belief in the werewolf. Giant supernatural wolves were thought to dig up graves at night to eat the people buried there. The werewolf was believed to be transformed by God as a punishment for not going to mass for seven years. He would roam the forest each night until blessed by a priest or killed by a silver bullet.

Newspaper reports in July and December, 1767, told of a werewolf that was seen in the area of Saint Roche, Quebec. During the day he was supposed to be a beggar and at night he was said to change into a giant bloodthirsty wolf.

The Nootka wolf cults

▲Each winter, during a full moon, the Indians of the north-west coast of America initiate young warriors into secret wolf cults. The Nootka tribe call this ceremony the 'Kulwana' and members of the society act the part of wolves. They wear a blanket tied at the forehead to form a snout because the wolf mask like the one above may only be worn by a chief. Young Nootkas are tested for endurance and bravery.

The Nootkas have a myth about the origins of the 'Kulwana'. They say that four brothers fled to Nootka Island when their tribe was wiped out in a war with neighbours. The youngest, Ha-Sass, sought knowledge from the wolves, who were said to know everything. He disguised himself in a seal skin, draining his blood so the wolves would not smell his human scent. The wolves found him and took him to their lair to eat.

When Ha-Sass revealed himself they admired his cunning so much that they taught him the wolf dances and rituals so he would become strong like them. The wolves wore masks of men (pictured left) for these magic ceremonies. After four days of training they gave Ha-Sass an enchanted club and sent him home to teach his brothers and other young men the secrets of the wolf power.

The Navaho wolf-men

The Navaho Indians of the south-western USA had a strong belief in magic and witchcraft and a great fear of the dead. Witches often dug up corpses to steal the treasures buried with them and take parts of dead bodies to make into magic poisons.

Witches were called 'human wolves' as they disguised themselves with mountain lion and wolf-skins. Some were even thought to turn into animals. The story here is an old Navaho legend about the terrible human wolves.

1. A Navaho girl and her small brother were travelling to fetch corn for their family. The girl knew they were being followed by human wolves so she sent her brother home on the horse. She hid in a thicket but was discovered by the human wolves.

2. The girl's oldest brother was hunting nearby and heard the wolves howling and his sister screaming. By the time he reached the thicket she had been carried away by the human wolves. He found bloody tracks and decided to follow them.

3. These tracks led to an opening in the face of a cliff. The boy entered and found a long dark passage cut from the stone. It went deep into the cliff and led to a cave full of human wolves. The boy hid in a small room littered with bones and treasure.

4. The human wolves soon found the boy and took him to their chief, who was large and fat, singing a song. He said the boy must either be put to death or become a human wolf. The boy decided to join them and try to escape later. They gave him some meat to eat. He knew it was human flesh, but did not know it came from his sister's body. She had been eaten by the human wolves, who had thrown her bones into a corner. He hid the meat, planning to feed it to the guard dogs later.

5. The boy waited for everyone to fall asleep, then crept past the dogs. The passage had been blocked but he managed to get outside and hide in a badger hole. The human wolves chased the boy but he was so well hidden they did not see him.

6. Two days later the boy reached home and learned of his sister's murder by the human wolves. On his way to the next war dance, he saw the human wolf chief riding a horse. The boy shot an arrow into his back and the wolf chief was killed.

Relatives of the werewolf

There are stories of people changing into almost every known animal, from sheep and birds to insects and fish. Any animal that was once a human is called a werebeast.

The transformations were not always evil, as with the werewolf.

Some took place after death, when the spirit returned to Earth as an animal. Some people even believed that animals could turn themselves into human beings if they wanted to.

The werefoxes of China and Japan were animals that became humans to trick and harm ordinary people. To do this a fox had to be 500 years old and live in a graveyard.

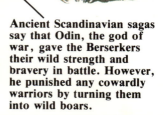

Ancient Scandinavian sagas say that Odin, the god of war, gave the Berserkers their wild strength and bravery in battle. However, he punished any cowardly warriors by turning them into wild boars.

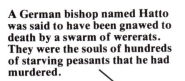

A German bishop named Hatto was said to have been gnawed to death by a swarm of wererats. They were the souls of hundreds of starving peasants that he had murdered.

Welsh witches were supposed to change into hares and drink all the milk from cows, leaving them dry when the farmer tried to milk them. They were also accused of casting evil spells that turned innocent people into animals, and of becoming man-eating werewolves when they died.

A sad Norwegian legend tells how Prince Bjorn terrorized the country as a huge bear, after being transformed by his wicked stepmother. He ate so many sheep that his father sent hunters to kill him, not realizing the bear was his own son. The stepmother cooked the body and served it at a celebration banquet.

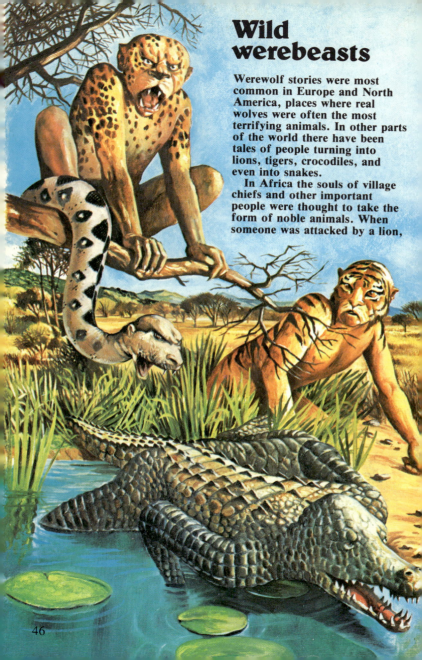

Wild
werebeasts

Werewolf stories were most
common in Europe and North
America, places where real
wolves were often the most
terrifying animals. In other parts
of the world there have been
tales of people turning into
lions, tigers, crocodiles, and
even into snakes.

In Africa the souls of village
chiefs and other important
people were thought to take the
form of noble animals. When
someone was attacked by a lion,

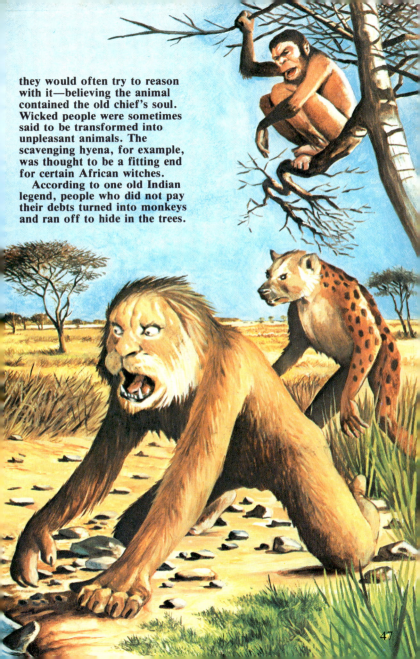

they would often try to reason
with it—believing the animal
contained the old chief's soul.
Wicked people were sometimes
said to be transformed into
unpleasant animals. The
scavenging hyena, for example,
was thought to be a fitting end
for certain African witches.

According to one old Indian
legend, people who did not pay
their debts turned into monkeys
and ran off to hide in the trees.

47

Introducing demons

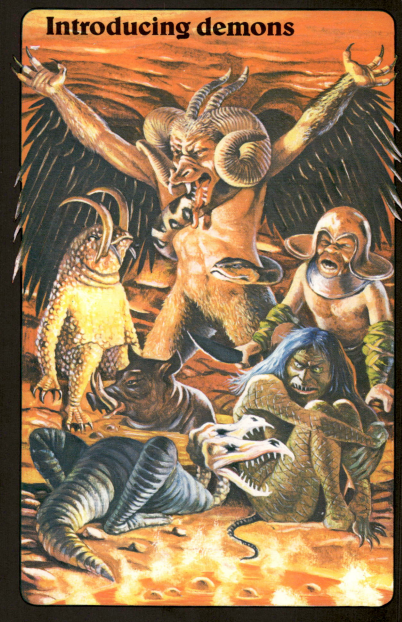

European vampires and werewolves, though supernatural and evil, were at least partly human. People became vampires or werewolves, so it was said, as a result of their wicked actions. The kind of spirit that encouraged evil was often more bizarre than the vampires or werewolves themselves.

For many years spirits called demons or devils were blamed for many of the misfortunes of life. Demons were not ghosts, as they had never been living human beings. Some people thought they were angels that had been expelled from heaven for rebelling against God. Others simply said they were elemental spirits—a form of supernatural life that took pleasure in destroying all that was good in the world.

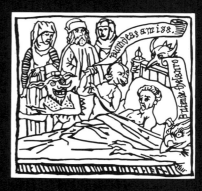

not always successfully.

Though demons were interested in influencing the world of the living, they were even more keen on gaining control of a person's soul after death. The rather gruesome illustration at the top of the page shows some demons waiting at the bedside of a dying person. They were supposed to drag the soul down to hell as the last breath was drawn.

Though many demons lived in hell, where they were said to thrive in a world of flames and tortured souls, they were seen by ordinary mortals during the hours of darkness. Sometimes demons offered a lifetime free from money worries in return for a person's soul. People who sold their souls to the devil signed a contract using their own blood as ink. Once this was done they could not escape unless a priest was able to release them from the devil's power with a prayer.

The illustration above shows a medieval demon playing on a trumpet to attract the attention of possible converts to his evil ways. Angels were supposed to protect people from demons, and they too played music, but

Some of the more mischievous demons were said to jump into the open mouths of people when they yawned. The only way to get the demon out of someone was to ask a priest to sprinkle holy water on the poor sufferer.

49

Medieval demons

Here are some of the many demons that were believed to haunt Europe throughout the Middle Ages. They ranged from evil old women, said to be witches, to dragons.

This Scandinavian dragon was called 'Niohoggr', which means 'Corpse tearer'. He was believed to carry off the dead with his sharp claws, devouring them in his lair deep beneath the earth.

Red Caps were bloodthirsty Scottish elves. They kept their caps red by dipping them in blood, obtained by throwing big boulders at passers-by.

During the plague-ridden Middle Ages, Death was pictured as a grinning human skeleton. He came suddenly to take people from the things they loved most.

People also believed the air was inhabited by over seven million demons. They haunted at night, could easily be swallowed, and animated corpses as vampires.

Demons formed an army of evil under the leadership of the devil. Each regiment had a captain; this one is Eurynome, the prince of death, who fed on human corpses.

Witches were thought to have magic powers from the devil. They spread disease, conjured up storms, changed into animal shapes and became vampires.

51

Demon ghosts and gods

Some demons were gods, like Kali and Xipe Totec, shown here, who could be very evil.

It is because demons were supposed to be beyond the laws of nature that they could create their bodies out of thin air or disguise themselves either as humans or animals.

▲This is Xipe Totec, a Mexican demon with a taste for blood. He was said to suck it from sinners who fell asleep in hell and the prisoners of war bled to death in sacrifice to him. Xipe Totec was believed to appear on earth wherever blood was spilt.

◄Kali is the Hindu Goddess of destruction, plague and violent death. Here she is holding the head of Raktivira, the king of the demons. He and Kali fought a savage battle, but Kali managed to kill Raktivira by stabbing him and drinking all his blood.

▶In the Caribbean Islands some vultures, known as Loogaroos, were said to be the ghosts of evil witches who had made pacts with the devil. He gave the witches magic powers while they were alive but when they died forced them to provide him with a daily supply of fresh blood.

At night the vultures removed their skins and flew off as spirits in search of victims. If the Loogaroo skin was found it was ground up with pepper and salt so the witch could not put it on and would be destroyed.

▶This strange creature is one of the Rakshasas. They were evil Indian demons that haunted burial grounds, animated dead bodies and terrorized priests. Rakshasas had great supernatural powers and could transform themselves into any shape they liked. Often they took on ugly deformed bodies with a crazy mixture of limbs in odd colours like blue, yellow, red or green.

These bloodthirsty demons were extremely dangerous. Their long nails were poisonous and they loved to eat human flesh, and sometimes even each other.

◀This Japanese demon also liked to eat people. It is one of the Kappas that lived in rivers and lakes and pulled into the water anyone silly enough to get close to them. There were only two ways of escaping a Kappa's jaws. The first was to feed it cucumber or melon, which Kappas loved so much they did not bother with tasteless humans. The other was by bowing to it. The Kappas were so polite they always bowed back, spilling the liquid stored in the top of their heads, which gave them their supernatural powers.

▶The Yara-Ma were demons which haunted the forests of Australia. They were small creatures, with scaly red and green skin and suckers instead of hands and feet. They hid in the branches of trees waiting for someone to sit in the shade beneath. Then the Yara-Ma leaped down, fixed its suckers to the victim, and drank his blood.

They had such huge mouths they could swallow a human being in one gulp. Occasionally, if the Yara-Ma went to sleep after his meal, his dinner might manage to climb out and run away.

'Vampires' from history

History is full of blood-thirsty tyrants, though perhaps none so frightening as Prince Vlad Dracula, or the Countess Elizabeth of Bathory.

Their histories read like the vampire legends of central Europe come to life.

Vlad the impaler

For part of the 15th century Prince Vlad Dracula ruled a small country called Wallachia. It is now part of the region of Transylvania in Romania. Bram Stoker probably based his fictional vampire count on Vlad Dracula, who was feared throughout Europe for his bloodthirsty deeds.

We know a great deal about Vlad Dracula's life and adventures as they were widely reported at the time and many of these records still survive.

He was usually known as 'Vlad the Impaler', a nickname he earned by impaling thousands of people on wooden stakes. This is a particularly nasty form of execution as the stakes were oiled and rounded at the ends. This way they did not cause gaping wounds and so death was slow and very painful.

He was also accused of skinning, roasting, boiling and chopping up people as if they were ingredients for a stew, and even of feeding the remains to the victims' families. It is said that he nailed hats to the heads of nobles who refused to remove them in respect for his rank.

In spite of his evil behaviour Dracula was sometimes described in Wallachia as a 'cruel but just ruler'. He was even seen as a hero because he drove out the Turkish armies that invaded Europe during the 15th century.

After one battle against Turkish invaders, Prince Dracula impaled an entire detachment of prisoners. On another occasion, he had 300 prisoners burned alive. In 1476, at the age of 46, Vlad was beheaded and buried in a monastery.

Elizabeth of Bathory

In 1611 the Hungarian countess Elizabeth of Bathory was bricked into one room of her castle as a punishment for killing over 650 young girls. She had murdered them for their blood which she bathed in, believing it would restore her youth and beauty.

The countess was very vain and feared growing old and losing the beauty for which she was famed throughout Europe. She discovered the magic blood cure when she hit a maid so hard that blood gushed from her nose all over Elizabeth's face and hands. She was convinced the blood had made her skin more lovely and decided to bath her whole body in it. The unfortunate maid was killed and her blood drained into a tub and gently warmed. This was the start of ten years of cruel murders for the hundreds of girls lured to the castle by promises of money and jobs. Instead, they were locked up and tortured, kept alive for as long as possible to be milked of their blood at dawn for the countess's beauty baths.

▼ Bran castle is close to the scene of one of Vlad Dracula's most bloodthirsty massacres. It is visited today by tourists searching for the truth about the Dracula legend.

Supernatural cinema

People love to be scared, which is why horror films are so very popular. They give a realistic setting to things we know are impossible.

On film we see the vampire in all his gory glory, fangs bared ready to sink into the throat of his next victim. Before our very eyes, a man turns into a furry wolf and lopes into the misty forest in search of human flesh. In the end good always triumphs over evil. The vampire is destroyed by a stake through the heart and the werewolf must be shot with a silver bullet.

▼ Bela Lugosi, the first famous screen Dracula, was actually born in Romania, traditional home of the vampire.

He began playing the Vampire Count in 1927 on the stage. A nurse was at every performance in case any of the audience were overcome by fright.

When he died in 1956, Bela Lugosi was buried wrapped in the black cloak, lined with red satin, that he had worn so often as Dracula.

The Prince of Darkness

An English company, Hammer Films, became the leading makers of horror films in the mid 1950s. They re-made many old horror classics in colour, using spectacular special effects and a great deal more blood than had been seen before.

Christopher Lee succeeded Bela Lugosi as the classic undead count after Hammer's first vampire film 'Dracula' was released in 1958.

On the right Christopher Lee is shown baring his fangs at his victims in the 1965 Hammer Films production 'Dracula, Prince of Darkness'. In this film the count is finally destroyed by being thrown into the ice-covered moat of his castle.

'Nosferatu'

This is the Vampire Count dissolving in a shaft of dawn sunlight in the first film version of Bram Stoker's novel 'Dracula'. The title of the film, made in 1922, was 'Nosferatu'—a Romanian word meaning the undead.

Movie horrors

Horror films have been made about many strange creatures besides vampires, including machine-like monsters and all kinds of werebeasts.

The picture below shows a zombie leaving his grave in the 1966 Hammer film 'Plague of the Zombies'. A zombie is a corpse brought to life by magic to act as a slave for its master.

In this film, set in south-west England, a local landowner puts an army of zombies to work in his tin mines. Instead of providing free labour, the zombies are blown to bits in an explosion when the squire's plans are foiled by the hero.

▲This snake woman from Hammer's film 'The Reptile' is a normal girl turned into a huge snake by a curse. She eats living animals but prefers to feed on people and even kills her father before being burnt to death.

▲ 'The Legend of the Werewolf', made by Tyburn Films, is about a baby reared by wolves. He grows up as a wolf-man and transforms at each full moon. He commits many foul murders, until he is hunted down and shot.

Monster make-up

The stars of horror films have to wear strange make-up in order to appear gruesome.

Vampires are dusted with a green powder to produce a corpse-like complexion. Their fake fangs are specially made by dentists. Christopher Lee wore red-coloured contact lenses to make his eyes look wild and blood-filled.

The werewolf's make-up is even more difficult. When Lon Chaney Jr played 'The Wolf Man' in 1941, hundreds of yak hairs were glued to his face to create a wolfish effect. It took a whole day and 21 changes of make-up to film the sequence showing him change into a wolf-man.

Supernatural guide

In this section you will have read about many of the important characters in the supernatural world of vampires, werewolves and demons. On these pages we list some of the other nasty creatures of this strange world, as well as some of the plants and animals connected with these dreadful legends.

BAT: Vampire bats live in dark places such as caves or hollow trees in many parts of central and south America. They were named after the bloodsucking vampires of legend as they are nocturnal creatures and live on the blood of other animals.

Vampire bats rarely attack humans but as their bites are fairly painless they can often drink the blood of a sleeping animal without it realizing.

BRUXAS: A female vampire from Portugal who flew out at night in the form of a bird. She drank the blood of her own children and terrified lonely travellers.

DHAMPIR: According to ancient Transylvanian legends the son of a vampire, known as a dhampir, was the only person who could see or kill the invisible vampires.

DRACUL: This is the Romanian word for devil or dragon. Vlad the Impaler was called Dracula because his father's name was Dracul and putting an 'a' on the end of a Romanian word makes it mean 'son of'. 'Dracula', therefore, actually means 'Son of the Devil'.

FAMILIAR: The pet of a witch, kept specially to help her in magical rituals. The most usual kind of animal familiar was a cat. There are stories of witches using toads, blackbirds and almost every other kind of small animal, and even, sometimes, demons.

GARLIC: A relative of the onion plant that is often used for seasoning food. It has also been used in many different ways as a protection against evil spirits, including vampires. An ancient Islamic legend says that garlic sprang up on the spot where Satan first put his foot after being expelled from paradise.

HARPIES: These female monsters were winged hags said to haunt the ancient Greeks. They carried living people away to hell and devoured shipwrecked sailors.

ITZPAPALOTL: A frightening Aztec demon who was a cross between a woman and a butterfly. Stone knives surrounded her wings and her tongue itself was a knife. She also had a magic cloak which she used to change herself into a harmless-looking butterfly.

JARACACA: An evil Brazilian vampire in the form of a snake. It was said to steal a mother's milk while she was feeding her child. At the same time the Jaracaca would put its tail in the mouth of the child.

JIGAR-KHOR: This was one of the many blood-drinking witches and spirits that were said to haunt the jungles of India. Jigar-khors were female spirits that were supposed to be able to steal their victims' livers simply by staring at them while reciting a magic spell.

KELPIE: A Scottish demon in the shape of a horse. Anyone who found a Kelpie lurking by the bank of a river and tried to ride it across the water found it impossible to get off again. The Kelpie always drowned its victims before eating them.

LAMIA: A vampire-like demon with the face of a beautiful woman but the body of a snake. According to Greek legends, Lamia fattened up young men before she devoured them.

MANDRAKE: This small plant was thought to have evil powers, as it was said to grow beneath the gallows where it could be nourished by the flesh and blood of the criminal hanging above. It was dangerous to pick, as the plant let out a scream when pulled from the ground that killed anyone who heard it.

MARA: A Danish vampire that was a beautiful woman during the day—but who sucked the blood from young men at night. Anyone who fell in love with her would suffer terrible feelings of suffocation and strangling, but she could be frightened away by a knife.

NEED-FIRES: Fires that were supposed to be able to drive away evil spirits. They were lit during catastrophies of many kinds throughout the Middle Ages and especially at times of plague. Need-fires had to be started at night, either by rubbing two pieces of wood together or else with a lighted twig from another need-fire.

OWENGAS: Vampires from Guinea in Northern Africa that were the bad spirits of evil ancestors or of dead magicians in a physical form. Belief in owengas led to the practice of clearing up all spilt blood and destroying any blood-stained objects in order to deprive them of their food.

SATAN: According to the Jewish and Christian traditions, Satan was a senior angel who lead a revolt against God. For his punishment, he was sent to hell, from where he directs a battle against all that is good in the world.

STRIGES: These Greek demons flew about at night as birds and snatched sleeping children from their cradles to eat their flesh and drink their blood.

THAYE TASE: One type of Burmese demon known generally as tases. They appear especially when there is an epidemic of cholera or smallpox and haunt those who are about to die, by giggling and laughing at their victim's pain. Like vampires, they are said to be the souls of people who have died a violent death.

VAMPIRE: The word probably comes from an old Turkish word 'oupir', meaning 'bloodsucker'.

Apart from ordinary vampires, such as Arnold Paole and the fictional Count Dracula, we have shown 19 different types of vampire in this book. There are so many strange legends throughout the world, and the imaginations of superstitious people are so powerful, that there have probably been many more kinds of vampire than we have included here.

VRYKOLAKAS: In Greek vampire legends, this ugly creature is the corpse of an evil man brought to life by a devil. The vrykolakas sat on its sleeping victims and killed them by suffocation.

WILLS-O'-THE-WISP: Glowing lights that can sometimes be seen at night hovering above rotting vegetation. When plants decay they can give off a gas that burns of its own accord. Before they were properly understood, these lights were the subject of many strange superstitions.

According to one old Chinese legend, Wills-o'-the-wisp were vampire-like evil spirits that grew out of spilt blood, or out of the rotting wood of coffins. They were said to make people ill and to ruin crops by burning the ears of corn. Like vampires, they only came out at night.

WOLF: Once common throughout Europe and North America, this animal that has inspired so many strange legends is now limited to remote areas.

The last wild wolves in Britain were killed in the eighteenth century. Although they kill other animals, it is very rare for wolves to attack humans.

ZOTZ: A South American demon in the legends of the Mayan people. The Zotz was an ugly winged creature with the head of a dog. It lived in a part of hell and drank the blood of anyone who passed through its territory.

Vampire quiz

Now that you have read all about vampires, werewolves and demons, test your knowledge by trying to answer these questions. The answers are at the bottom of the next page. They are printed upside down and back to front to make cheating more difficult. In order to read them, hold the page upside down in front of a mirror.

1 Who thought that vampires left their bones behind in the grave?
2 Name four things which give protection against vampires.
3 Why should werewolves be burned rather than buried after they die?
4 What rare disease makes its victims appear to be dead?
5 Who is the Hindu Goddess of destruction, violent death and plague?
6 Who were the 'Ressurection Men'? What did they do?
7 What do Kappas like to eat even better than humans?
8 What time of day do most vampires leave their graves?
9 Which vampire could turn into a cat, toad or any sort of bloodsucking insect?
10 Who took beauty baths in human blood every morning?
11 Which bloodthirsty Scottish elves threw large boulders at travellers?
12 What were werewolves said to do with their fur while in human shape?
13 Which vampires floated in blood-filled coffins?
14 What is the name given to a corpse brought to life by magic, to act as a slave for its master?

15 What Scottish demon had the shape of a horse?
16 What did the Navaho Indians call evil witches?
17 Who wrote the novel 'Dracula'?
18 What plant was said to grow under gallows and feed on the blood of hanged criminals?
19 What is the pelesit vampire of Malaya created out of?
20 What are the best things to kill a werewolf with?
21 How many demons were said to inhabit the air during the Middle Ages?
22 Which flowers were buried with vampires to prevent them returning from the grave?
23 Where was the murony vampire said to be found?
24 Which bishop was supposed to have been gnawed to death by a swarm of wererats?
25 According to Indian legend, what did people who did not pay their debts turn into?
26 When people sold their soul to the devil what did they use as ink on the contract?
27 What was drinking the water that collected in a wolf's paw print said to do?
28 Which vampire had two sorts of body?

29	Where do most vampires bite their victims?	37	Why were vampires buried with garlic in their mouths?
30	Which vampire could become an owl?	38	What vampire sits on its victims and suffocates them?
31	What was Prince Vlad Dracula usually known as?	39	What is the illness which makes people think they are werewolves?
32	Which film actor was buried in his Dracula cloak?	40	How do you destroy a Loogaroo's vulture skin?
33	How many tails did Japanese vampire cats have?	41	What were the symptoms caused by a bajang attack?
34	What Mayan demon was said to live in Hell, have the head of a dog and drink blood?	42	Which Norse god was said to give the Berserkers their great strength in battle?
35	What is a Dhampir?	43	Which vampire gnawed his own hands and feet?
36	Who turned Prince Bjorn of Norway into a bear?	44	What did the name of the dragon Niohoggr mean?

Answers

1 European gypsies.

2 Wild roses, garlic, lilac, lime and crosses.

3 To stop them becoming vampires.

4 Caterpillar vampires.

5 Kali.

6 Body snatchers who sold corpses to doctors.

7 Cucumbers and melons.

8 A snake.

9 The mummy.

10 Countess Elisabeth Bathory.

11 The Red Caps.

12 Keep it on the inside of their skin.

13 Polish vampires.

14 A vampire.

15 The Kelpie.

16 Human wolves.

17 Bram Stoker.

18 The mandrake.

19 The tongue of a dead dog.

20 A bullet or knife made badly, or silver from a crucifix.

21 Seven million.

22 Wild roses.

23 In Transylvania.

24 Bishop Hatto.

25 Monkeys.

26 Their own blood.

27 Turn you into a werewolf.

28 The Bulgarian vampire.

29 In the neck.

30 The langsuir.

31 Vlad the Impaler.

32 Bela Lugosi.

33 Two.

34 The Zotz.

35 The son of a vampire.

36 His stepmother.

37 To stop them biting.

38 The Vrykolakas.

39 Lycanthropy.

40 Grinding it with salt and pepper.

41 Fainting and convulsions.

42 Odin.

43 The Russian Viesczy.

44 Corpse tearer.

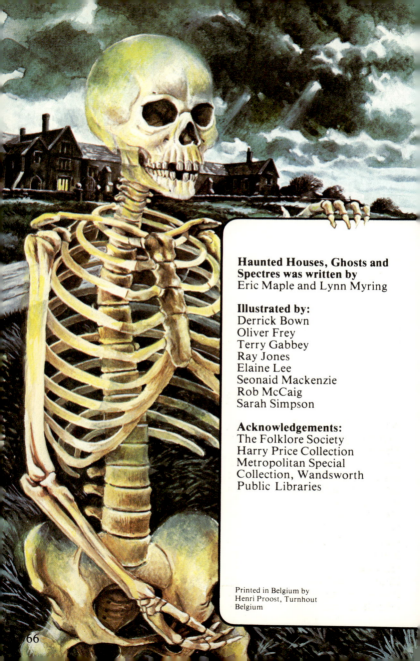

Haunted Houses, Ghosts and Spectres was written by
Eric Maple and Lynn Myring

Illustrated by:
Derrick Bown
Oliver Frey
Terry Gabbey
Ray Jones
Elaine Lee
Seonaid Mackenzie
Rob McCaig
Sarah Simpson

Acknowledgements:
The Folklore Society
Harry Price Collection
Metropolitan Special
Collection, Wandsworth
Public Libraries

Printed in Belgium by
Henri Proost, Turnhout
Belgium

Part 2

HAUNTED HOUSES GHOSTS & SPECTRES

Introduction

For hundreds of years people have believed that some houses are haunted. Ghostly figures have mysteriously appeared, and often vanished without trace.

This part contains over 70 stories of hauntings. It shows some of the ways people have tried to get rid of ghosts and it includes explanations, both natural and supernatural, of hauntings of all kinds. There are also stories of fake phantoms, and some ideas for taking your own 'ghost' photographs.

Contents

What is a haunted house?

Many houses appear to be the homes not only of living people, but also of some supernatural presence.

The ghostly inhabitant may make its presence felt in various ways. Sometimes it seems to be the spirit of someone who has died. People living in the house may hear moans or groans in the middle of the night, or the sound of voices or of footsteps when no-one else is present. They may see strange lights or misty, phantom shapes. They may see figures that seem entirely human— except for the lack of a head, or the ability to pass through walls.

Sometimes the disturbances in a haunted house may be non-human. There have been reports of mysterious smells, sudden draughts in closed rooms, and abrupt changes in temperature. Sometimes lights go on and off and objects move about, apparently of their own accord.

Sometimes the haunting stops as soon as a particular person stops living in the house. On other occasions, it proves necessary to call in an expert, usually a priest, who knows how to deal with a haunting.

Very often, investigation of the history of a haunted place reveals some terrible tragedy in its past. For this reason, many people believe that a haunting is caused because the spirit of someone connected with the place is Earth-bound, or unable to join the spirit world.

Few houses remain permanently haunted. Most are haunted only at special times of the year, and sometimes the spectre appears only once.

Many hauntings have been investigated thoroughly and some have been found to have natural explanations. Others remain unexplained, though we may discover causes for these at some time in the future.

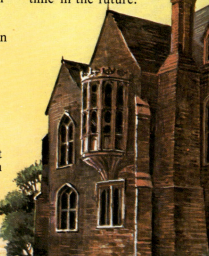

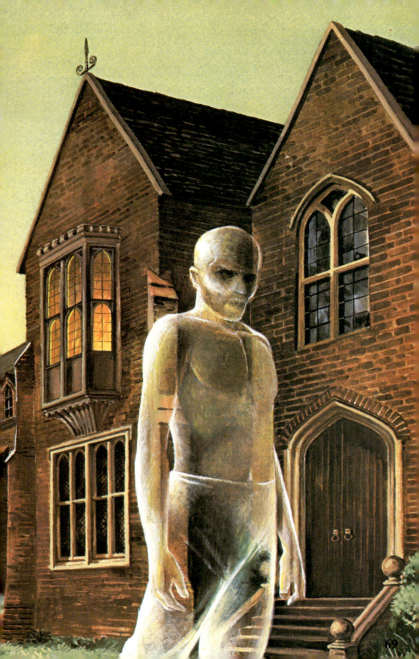

Types of ghost

Though most ghosts are reported to look something like people, there are many different types of haunting.

Some ghosts are not recognizable as phantoms because they look so solid and real. These are usually the ghosts of the newly dead. They most often appear to relatives or close friends just as they are dying.

Many ghosts are surrounded by a kind of glowing light like a halo or even by fire. Other apparitions are colourless and transparent. They can look as if they are part of the walls or the furniture of the rooms in which they appear.

On these pages you can see examples of some of the most common forms of haunting.

▶Not all ghosts are immediately visible, even to people who can hear them moving about.

Some years ago in Italy after a workman died, his friends heard the sound of footsteps in the workshop. They called in a photographer to check their suspicions that the building was haunted. Although no phantom was ever seen by the workers, a photograph taken in the middle of the night clearly showed the misty figure of a ghost. It was the dead workman, standing at his old bench, just as if he were alive.

◀An example of a fiery phantom was seen one night in Rome, in 1683. A man woke up to find the ghost of a woman standing by his bed. She was dressed in white and her whole body gave off a dazzling bright light that lit up the whole room.

The ghost began talking to the surprised man, as bright flames shot out from her body. 'Look where I touch,' she said, before vanishing into thin air. The bed cover had been burned and bore the scorched imprint of the ghost's right hand.

◄Some ghosts fade away as they grow older. In the 18th century a spectral woman wearing a red dress, red shoes and a black head-dress was seen in an old house. About 70 years later she was seen dressed in pink.

By the middle of the 19th century she had become a ghost in a white gown with grey hair. In 1939 the haunting was reduced to phantom footsteps and the swish of her dress and by 1971 her presence was merely sensed by workmen demolishing the house.

►Ghosts are very often thought of as shrouded figures, perhaps because of the white robes in which people were once buried.

King Charles I saw a shrouded spectre in 1645, during the English Civil War. It was the ghost of his loyal friend, the Earl of Strafford, who had recently been executed. He warned the king that he would lose the battle he planned for the next day. Charles ignored the ghostly advice, and the Royalists never recovered from the defeat they suffered in this battle.

◄Sometimes a place is haunted by machines, as well as people.

Abraham Lincoln's funeral train is said to haunt the route it took through New York State when carrying the president's body after he was killed in 1865.

Whenever the ghostly train passes through a station, all the clocks are said to stop. Lincoln has never been seen on the train (though his ghost has appeared in the White House), but a band of musicians in the form of skeletons has been seen on one of the train's wagons.

The most haunted house in the world?

In 1863 in the English village of Borley, about 100 km north-east of London, a rectory was built on the site of an old parsonage. It was to become famous as the home of a variety of ghosts and a huge number of strange happenings.

By 1939, when the house burned down, there had been over 200 reported sightings of ghosts. Nothing is left of the rectory today except many stories — and a host of unanswered questions.

1. Those who live in Borley village say that a phantom nun has haunted the area for centuries. She often used to wander through the grounds of the rectory and she can still be seen today, gliding along a path called 'Nun's Walk'.

2. When the Reverend Henry Bull had Borley Rectory built, he put a summer-house facing the Nun's Walk, so that he could sit and watch the nun. She startled people by peering in at them through the windows of the new house.

3. Many other strange things occurred at this time. A phantom coach and horses raced along the drive, bells rang and objects flew about the house, without any explanation. Voices, footsteps, figures, and even strange smells were reported.

4. In 1930 the Reverend Foyster and his wife Marianne moved in to the rectory. Soon afterwards disturbing words that looked like messages began to appear on the walls. One sentence said simply, 'Marianne please help get.'

5. Harry Price, an expert ghost hunter, rented the rectory for a year in 1937. A huge file of odd happenings, was built up by his team of 48 observers. They saw the nun walk on the lawn. Other ghostly shapes appeared to pass through walls.

6. In 1939 the rectory was destroyed by a fire. Ghosts looked on at the flames. People searching in the ruins saw lights, heard knockings and discovered inexplicable variations in temperature where the house used to stand.

7. Harry Price returned in 1943, to make further investigations. Digging in the cellar he found part of the jawbone of a young woman. He felt sure it was from the phantom nun, and gave it a Christian burial, in an attempt to end the hauntings.

Inside Borley Rectory

Almost every room in Borley Rectory seems to have been haunted. This diagram of the house shows where many of the strange occurrences took place.

Even today, when nothing is left on the site, the area is still said to be haunted by the phantom nun.

One part of the first floor landing was known as the 'cold spot'. When people stood there, they often felt extremely cold. Tests proved that the temperature here was sometimes as much as six degrees cooler than the surrounding air.

Ghostly footsteps were often heard up and down the rectory's main staircase. On one occasion a rector's wife was followed upstairs by the phantom of a former rector.

The ghosts seemed especially to enjoy hurling things down the stairs. Many ornaments and bottles which had vanished from locked rooms, were discovered smashed at the bottom of the staircase.

This study was Harry Price's base when he rented the rectory in 1937 in order to investigate the hauntings. One man, alone in the room, heard the key turn in the lock. He looked round and the door was still closed with the key on the inside, but the door was inexplicably locked. Whoever had locked the door must have been in the study with the investigator, although he saw no-one.

The bedrooms above the kitchens were haunted by unexplained footsteps. The doors seemed to lock and unlock themselves.

Even the bathroom was haunted. One woman going past the door was given a black eye when an invisible hand slapped her on the face. Mysterious 'spirit writing' appeared on the landing, just outside the bathroom.

This bedroom, known as the 'Blue Room' was the most haunted part of the house. Mysterious forces threw people out of bed. Objects rose into the air or vanished, while other things appeared out of nowhere. A gold ring and an old coat, that had never been seen before, were found here during one of Price's investigations in 1937.

In the kitchen, invisible ghosts sometimes threw crockery around. On one occasion, several wine bottles materialized in mid-air. They hovered for a few moments and then smashed to the ground. The bells that were used to call the servants often rang when no-one was using them. They even continued to ring after their wires had been disconnected.

Henry Bull had one of the windows in the dining room bricked up. This was because the phantom nun had begun to stare wistfully at the family while they were having their meals.

On Harry Price's first visit to the rectory in 1929, half a brick mysteriously smashed through the glass roof of the verandah, showering him with splinters of glass. At the time, the house was completely empty and locked up.

Ghosts of the living

People sometimes report having seen an apparition of a close friend or relative at a time when the person seen is actually far away.

These 'phantoms of the living' often try to tell those they visit that they are in trouble and need help.

One explanation is that the phantom figures are somehow produced by 'mental energy'. Other explanations include the possibility that people have two bodies: an ordinary physical one and a ghost-like spirit which only escapes at times of crisis.

▲In 1944 the ghostly figure of a paratrooper appeared in a house in England. It was later discovered that, at the time his ghost appeared to his friend at home, the paratrooper had been seriously wounded in battle in Holland.

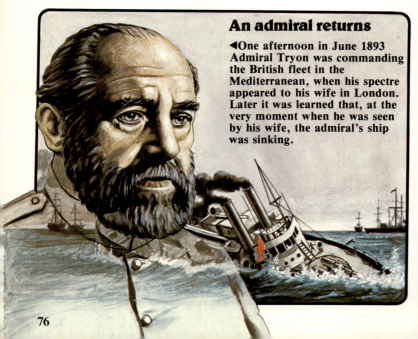

An admiral returns

◀One afternoon in June 1893 Admiral Tryon was commanding the British fleet in the Mediterranean, when his spectre appeared to his wife in London. Later it was learned that, at the very moment when he was seen by his wife, the admiral's ship was sinking.

A phantom warning

In one strange case, the arrival of a phantom of a living man served, years later, to save the life of another man.

The story began during the 1880s. Lord Dufferin was staying in a country house in Ireland when he woke up one night to see a ghostly figure outside the window. It was moving across the lawn, carrying a coffin on its back.

Lord Dufferin ran out to the garden and asked the man what he was doing. The mysterious figure raised its ghastly face and suddenly vanished.

◄Ten years later, Lord Dufferin was the British Ambassador to France. One afternoon Lord Dufferin and his family were attending a reception at the Grand Hotel in Paris. Dufferin was just about to enter the lift, when he recognized the lift operator as the phantom he had seen carrying a coffin in Ireland.

Completely shocked, Lord Dufferin refused to enter the lift. A moment later it crashed to the bottom of its shaft, killing all its passengers. Nobody could discover why the lift had suddenly failed, but Dufferin believed the ghost had saved his life.

Poltergeists

Poltergeists are not ghosts in the ordinary sense. They are invisible hauntings, only known about because of the strange disturbances they cause. Poltergeists are blamed for objects flying through the air or things suddenly appearing from nowhere. Some poltergeists are said to make things break into little pieces or become very hot or very cold.

Poltergeist activity is most often observed when there are children aged between 12 and 16 living in a house. The word 'poltergeist' comes from the German for noisy spirit.

▲In 1821 a farm in Tennessee, USA, was haunted by a poltergeist that hurled clods of earth at children and pulled their hair. It sang songs at the farmer's funeral and after many disturbances, it disappeared, shouting, 'Goodbye'.

The Battersea spirit

In November, 1927 a poltergeist began to haunt a house in Battersea, London. First it caused showers of coal and coins to fall out of thin air. Windows smashed for no reason and furniture began to fly about the rooms.

An 86 year-old invalid was upstairs in bed when, shortly after the hauntings began, the window of his room blew in,

together with its frame. It was as
if a bomb had exploded.

Harry Price, the man who
later investigated Borley
Rectory, was called in to
examine the house. The havoc
continued but no explanation
could be found. Chairs even
marched down the hall and piled
themselves up onto a table,
before the poltergeist eventually
disappeared.

▲In the late 1960s a building in
Kilakee, Ireland was invaded by
hats of all types. They appeared
overnight without explanation.
Bells began to ring, glue
appeared on the walls and the
furniture was smashed to pieces.
The mystery was never solved.

▲One 17th century English
poltergeist made books and
furniture fly around the house.
A drum that had been taken
from a poor beggar by the
owner of the house began to
beat on its own. The children of
the house had their hair pulled.

Headless ghosts

Perhaps one of the most terrifying experiences that can be imagined is the sight of a person without a head.

Wherever there are stories of ghosts, there are stories of headless phantoms. Beheading used to be a common form of execution, especially for important prisoners. This may account for the large number of headless royal ghosts.

It used to be thought that a soul could not attend the day of judgement unless its body was complete. One explanation for headless phantoms is that they haunt the world of the living in an attempt to find their heads.

Headless horses have also been seen—pulling phantom coaches down country lanes.

The headless lady of Echt

The crossroads at Echt in Holland have been haunted for centuries by a headless woman, known as the Lady of Echt.

She hovers over the spot where a hoard of treasure is supposed to lie buried. She is condemned to haunt the site until the gold is given to the poor.

The Lady of Echt once offered a third of the treasure to a young man to dig it up. She warned him that he must keep silent while working. Unfortunately, when the man's spade hit the lid of the treasure chest, he cried out, 'Saints alive!' The chest promptly sank back into the ground and has never been seen since.

▲A terrifying headless woman haunts a marsh on the east coast of England at dusk. She wears a bonnet, but it is completely empty and no head or face can be seen. Anyone who gets in her way is swept into a whirlwind that passes behind her.

▲Dover Castle is haunted by a headless drummer boy, who walks the battlements at night. He is said to be the ghost of a young drummer, found dead in mysterious circumstances at the end of the 18th century, when the castle was rebuilt.

▲A soldier who had his head blown off during the War of Independence in the USA still haunts the scene of his death. His ghost gallops wildly on a phantom horse through Greenburgh, by the Hudson River, searching for its head.

▲This bodyless head is perhaps looking for its headless body. The head was seen by German farm-hands in the 19th century, when it flew into a barn. It predicted the death of one of the farm-hand's sisters. The girl drowned later that day.

Ghosts with a purpose

Some hauntings appear to be just the aimless wanderings of a lost spirit, but many ghosts are said to return because they have some purpose to fulfil on Earth.

Often a ghost returns in order to pass on information to the living. Sometimes the news is good news; a surprising number of stories are connected with finding money. Many spectres warn people of danger. Other ghosts seek to right a wrong or to make sure that a promise made during their lifetime is carried out.

▲During World War I a phantom sentry once appeared and stopped an ambulance. The sentry vanished and the driver got out. Just ahead was a huge hole in the road. Without the ghost, the ambulance would have crashed.

▲A phantom woman appeared to a man walking past a Polish cemetery. She told him that she could not rest, as her child had been buried unbaptized. The ghost vanished after a priest had blessed the grave the ghost had pointed to.

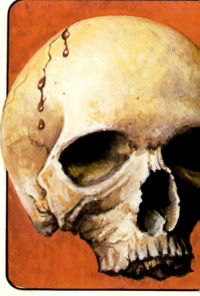

▲In 1964 a Detroit car worker was saved from certain death by a ghost. A machine almost crushed him, but at the last moment he was pulled out of the way—by the ghost of a man who had died in a similar accident 20 years before.

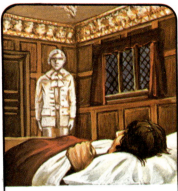

The screaming Skull

A human skull kept at Bettiscombe Manor in Dorset is said to scream if it is ever moved from the house.

The skull is supposed to be that of a negro slave brought from the West Indies in the 18th century. The slave was promised that when he died his body would be sent back to his homeland for burial, but the promise was broken and he was buried at Bettiscombe.

In its grave, the body began to scream, and it was dug up and kept in the manor house. Now, only the skull remains, but people say that it still screams—and that it has been known to sweat blood.

Soon after the death of Monsieur de Monteville, Dutch ambassador to Sweden in the 18th Century, his widow was troubled by a man who claimed that her late husband still owed him 25,000 Dutch Guilders. The woman went for help to the Swedish mystic, Emmanual Swedenborg.

Shortly afterwards, the ambassador's ghost appeared to Swedenborg and told him he would visit his widow in a dream.

De Monteville's ghost soon appeared to his widow in a dream. He showed her where to find proof that he had paid the debt, together with a pile of money and a valuable diamond haircomb.

Ghosts and the famous

Throughout history there have been reports of famous men and women returning as phantoms to haunt the places where they lived.

One reason why there are so many stories about famous people returning as ghosts might be because so many of them were assassinated or died before they felt their life's work was done.

Another reason for the large number of ghosts connected with the famous is simply that people are very likely to remember any strange tale they hear about a famous man or woman.

▲The Roman emperor, Nero, was said to haunt the streets of Rome after he had fled from his enemies and committed suicide. The ghost disappeared after a church was built over Nero's tomb.

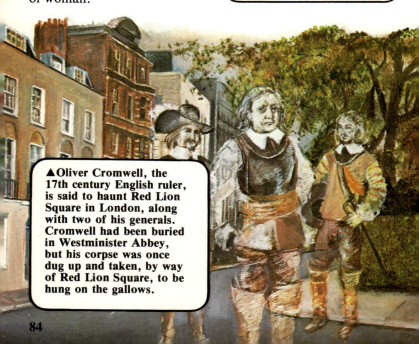

▲Oliver Cromwell, the 17th century English ruler, is said to haunt Red Lion Square in London, along with two of his generals. Cromwell had been buried in Westminister Abbey, but his corpse was once dug up and taken, by way of Red Lion Square, to be hung on the gallows.

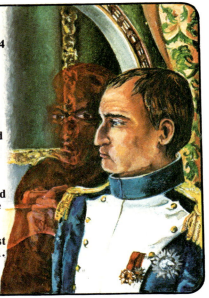

Napoleon Bonaparte, Emperor of France from 1804 to 1815, was very often followed by a ghostly red figure. Some people thought it was a ghost while others said it was a demon in disguise.

Like many ghosts, the Red Man was most often reported to appear at times of crisis—especially towards the end of a battle, just before a defeat.

Napoleon seriously believed that the dead could influence coming events. He often consulted a medium to seek advice about what to do. Just before his own death in 1821, Napoleon saw the ghost of his dead wife, Josephine.

The ghost of the American president Abraham Lincoln is believed to haunt the White House in Washington. President Theodore Roosevelt, Sir Winston Churchill and President Eisenhower are among those who have sensed Lincoln's presence.

One day the wife of President Lyndon Johnson was watching a television programme about Abraham Lincoln's assassination, when she felt something forcing her to look towards the mantelpiece. Her eyes were directed to a commemorative plaque on the wall above telling of Lincoln's connection with the room. As she read it, she felt a strange draught.

Royal ghosts

Throughout history there have been stories about the ghosts of kings and queens and princes.

Many monarchs were very cruel and were often the victims of violent deaths themselves. This fact, together with the mystery that surrounded kings and queens in the past, makes it hardly surprising that there should be lots of royal ghost stories.

The shortage of modern royal ghosts is probably because most of the world's royal families have ceased to exist.

▲The ghosts of Edward V and Richard, Duke of York, have been seen in the Tower of London. In 1483 the two Princes were murdered there. Two hundred years later their skeletons were found, and moved to Westminster Abbey.

The phantom wives of Henry VIII

King Henry VIII had six wives, at least four of whom have returned as ghosts.

Catherine of Aragon, Henry's first wife, has often been seen in a castle in Cambridgeshire. Anne Boleyn, Henry's second wife, was beheaded in 1536. Her ghost dressed in white has visited the houses where she lived, carrying her own head.

The ghost of Henry's third wife, Jane Seymour, haunts several houses holding a lighted taper.

Henry's fifth wife, Catherine Howard, was beheaded in 1542 for having a love affair with one of the court musicians. Her phantom has appeared in the room in Hampton Court Palace where she was arrested.

▲Queen Elizabeth I, who died in 1603, has since been seen walking along the walls of Windsor Castle, about 35 kilometres west of London. She is also said to haunt the library at Windsor, and was seen there only a few days after her death.

▲The ghost of George II has been seen gazing up at the weather vane on Kensington Palace, in London. When he died on October 25, 1760, he was waiting for messengers from Germany. His spirit is said to mutter, 'Why don't they come?'

Haunted castles

There are so many stories of haunted castles, it is hard to believe that they can all be true. Nearly every castle in Britain, and many on the mainland of Europe, are said to be haunted.

Castle ghosts are said to be the victims of past horrors. The cavernous dungeons ancient castles were very often the setting for grisly torture and violent death.

Crathies

Crathes Castle, not far from Aberdeen in Scotland, is haunted by one of the most chilling sights of all. The massive building was completed in 1594 and from that date until 1966 remained the home of the Burnard family.

Over the centuries there have been many reports of a phantom woman who creeps across one of the rooms. The ghostly figure, who is always dressed in green, moves across the old room and plucks a phantom baby out of the fireplace.

Some years ago, the bones of a woman and child were discovered hidden beneath the ancient fireplace.

Blandy

The Chateau at Blandy, not far from Paris, was said to be one of the most haunted castles in France.

According to legend, a group of phantoms appears on All Saints Day (November 1). They fly around the castle walls and land on the round tower. Villagers have also reported the sound of ghostly chains rattling and frightening screams coming from underground.

Another of the ghosts of Blandy is Count Dunois, a former lord of the castle. He is sometimes seen mounted on his horse, wearing a suit of armour.

Glamis

Glamis Castle (pronounced 'Glaams') in north-east Scotland is the home of ten ghosts. One of the most horrific sights that has been reported is a phantom lady without a tongue. She has been seen running across the park, screaming, as she points to her bleeding mouth.

In the nearby village of Glamis there are stories of the ghost of Malcolm II, an 11th century king of Scotland, who is said to haunt the graveyard.

Other Glamis ghosts include the tall figure of a local lord. He was playing cards one night in the castle when the devil appeared and they both vanished in a puff of smoke.

Phantom battles

There have been many reports of ghosts appearing over the sites where great battles were fought.

Battlefield ghosts almost always appear as spectral armies. This is unusual, as most other hauntings involve individual ghosts—and are connected with suicides or isolated murders. Phantom battles, unlike most hauntings, are often seen by more than one person at a time.

It remains a mystery why most phantom battles are fought in the skies above the original battleground.

▲One of the bloodiest battles of the English Civil War was at Edgehill in 1642. On Christmas Eve the same year, and many times since, phantom armies of King Charles and Cromwell have been seen fighting above the battleground.

The battle of Marathon

▶One of the earliest phantom battles was fought between masses of ghostly Greek and Persian soldiers over the plains of Marathon. The apparitions were first sighted soon after the Greek victory in the real battle of Marathon in 490BC.

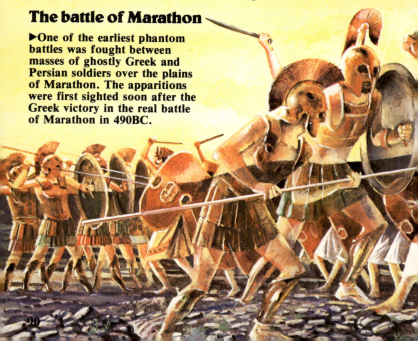

▲A few weeks after Napoleon's final defeat at the Battle of Waterloo in June 1815, the people of Verviers in Belgium witnessed a ghostly re-enactment of the famous battle. Phantom cavalry and the sound of cannon thundered across the skies.

▲One day in August 1951, two women on the north coast of France were woken by the sound of guns firing and aircraft attacking. They appear to have heard a ghostly re-enactment of the Allies' raid on Dieppe that took place in August 1942.

Phantom transport

For centuries there have been reports of hauntings along the tracks, lanes and highways of the world. Once there were ghostly horsemen and phantom coaches. Now there are spectral cars and lorries, phantom trains and ghostly hitch-hikers, and sightings of all kinds of mysterious vehicles.

According to some, hauntings are most likely to occur if someone has suffered a violent or untimely death, and any means of transport is a potential killer.

▲A ghostly cyclist who rides along an English country lane in Essex causes a great deal of fright and even near- accidents. He appears at dusk, on an old-fashioned bicycle without any lights, and rides straight at anyone in the road.

▲A woman driving along a quiet road once saw a phantom car go through a closed gate in a hedge and over a deep ditch, without causing any damage. It then vanished without trace.

▲Whenever there is a thunderstorm over Weybridge in Surrey, England, people report the sound of a biplane.

It is said to carry the ghost of an airman, killed in 1935 during a similar storm.

The train that disappeared

On December 28, 1879, the Tay rail bridge in Scotland was wrecked by a violent gale. The middle section was blown down, leaving a gaping hole in place of the track.

The night train from Edinburgh, rushing across the bridge on its way to Dundee, plunged into the River Tay, killing all the crew and 78 passengers on board. Soon after the accident, rumours began that the bridge was haunted by those who died that night.

The Tay bridge was rebuilt and opened again in 1887, but this did not stop the hauntings. Many years after the disaster, a man named Smith saw a steam train crossing the bridge from the Edinburgh side. It was travelling very fast with headlights blazing, but was totally silent and vanished near the centre of the bridge. Mr Smith was puzzled and, on investigation, found that no train had crossed the bridge at the time he had seen one. But the date of this phantom train's appearance was December 28— the anniversary of the Tay Bridge disaster.

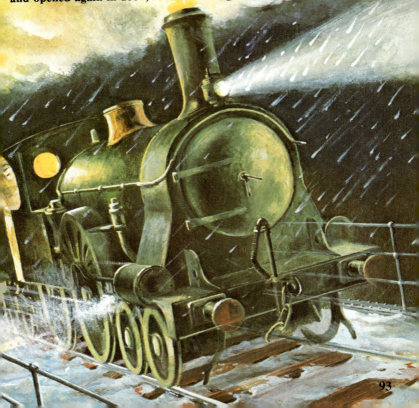

Ghosts at sea

There are many superstitions connected with sailors who die at sea. Because they often do not have a proper burial, there are many stories of sailors haunting the seas.

According to one legend, the souls of drowned sailors return as seagulls, and no sailor should ever shoot one of these birds.

▼ In February 1748 a ship called the Lady Luvibond sailed down the Thames from London, with a cargo for Portugal. One sailor apparently went mad. He murdered the helmsman and took over the wheel. The mad sailor steered the Luvibond onto a sandbank in the Straits of Dover and the ship soon sank into the sands.

Fifty years later, the ghost of the Luvibond was seen breaking-up on the sands. It has reappeared every 50 years on the anniversary of its sinking.

▲The captain of an 18th century slaver once murdered a sailor and had his body fed to the slaves as a stew. The sailor soon came back as a ghost to haunt the captain. The terrified captain threw himself overboard.

▲In 1959, two British naval ships went to the rescue of a landing craft that was seen in distress off the coast of Devon. When they drew near the craft, which was flying the flag of the wartime Free French navy, it vanished.

►A wild corner of the north-west coast of Scotland is haunted by the ghost of a tall sailor. He wanders along the shore, leaving no footprints in the sand. Many years ago the body of a tall ship-wrecked sailor was found, which looked like the phantom.

Haunted mountains

The icy peaks of mountains seem to be strangely haunted. Mountaineers report odd visions and sensations—one of the commonest is a sense that they are being followed.

These may be caused by the peculiar intensity of the sunlight on the snow, or by the moaning of the wind in the deep silence. But many events remain unexplained.

The ghost that climbed on Everest

It was September 26, 1975, nearly dawn on the moonlit crags of Everest. Mountaineer Nick Estcourt, of the Bonington expedition, struggled up the ropes that linked Camps 4 and 5. As he reached 300 metres above Camp 4, he saw a figure climbing after him. He could just make out the dark limbs against the bright snow. It looked as though another climber had set out earlier than planned.

When he telephoned from Camp 5, Estcourt was told that no-one had left Camp 4. Later that day, Mick Burke, a television cameraman with the team, died in a lone climb to the summit of Everest.

When Chris Bonington, the leader of the expedition, returned to Britain, he was handed a strange letter. It had been written early in 1975 by a clairvoyant named Clement Williamson, and then locked in a bank vault for safe-keeping. It contained a message Williamson had 'received' from a climber named Andrew Irvine, who had disappeared on Mount Everest in 1924.

The message predicted that on the Bonington expedition a ghost would appear and that someone would die.

▲The Great Grey Man haunts Ben Macdhui, the highest peak in the Scottish Cairngorms. Once, in 1943, a mountaineer even fired his revolver at the huge human shape. The spectre remained unharmed and the climber fled in terror.

▲This vision appeared in 1865 to a climber on the Matterhorn in the German Alps. It was not a supernatural sign, but an illusion, called a 'fogbow', made by sunlight on the clouds.

Animal apparitions

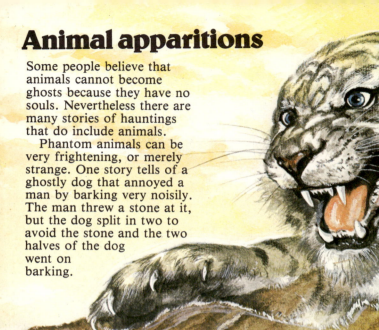

Some people believe that animals cannot become ghosts because they have no souls. Nevertheless there are many stories of hauntings that do include animals.

Phantom animals can be very frightening, or merely strange. One story tells of a ghostly dog that annoyed a man by barking very noisily. The man threw a stone at it, but the dog split in two to avoid the stone and the two halves of the dog went on barking.

▲French soldiers who slept in a ruined house in Morocco soon found that it was haunted. A horrific scream woke them at midnight and a huge black phantom hound suddenly materialized. The dog leapt over the soldiers and then vanished.

▲The ghost of a wild stallion, known as the White Devil, haunts the American prairies. When alive, the rogue horse had protected a herd of wild horses by biting and stamping on anyone who tried to catch them.

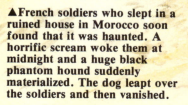

The leper's curse

◀In India during the 1880s, a blind leper asked Charles de Silva for protection from a tiger that was terrorizing the jungle. De Silva ran off and the tiger attacked the leper. In revenge, the leper put a curse on de Silva.

News soon came of a tiger that had turned white with leprosy. De Silva hoped that by killing the tiger he could break the curse, but a few days after its death, the tiger's ghost attacked his wife and son. Although only a phantom, the tiger killed two people: De Silva's son died of leprosy and his nanny died of fright. The leper's curse had been fulfilled.

▲Some Canadian Indians believe that if they feed the bones of a beaver they catch to their dogs, the ghost of the beaver becomes angry. The phantom beaver then returns to persuade its living relatives not to be caught by the Indians.

▲Hunters in Siberia hold a special festival in honour of every whale they kill. They hope that its ghost will tell the other whales how well it has been treated after being killed, so that they will not sink the hunting boats.

Hauntings in America

The Europeans who emigrated to the New World took with them their fears of ghosts and the supernatural. Life was tough and there were many killings, which often lead to rumours of hauntings.

The original inhabitants of America also had tales of ghosts. The last of the Mohawk Indians, who died in 1789, is said to paddle a ghostly canoe up and down the Mohawk river.

In more recent times there have been plagues of poltergeists and phantom cars.

▲In 1880 the Hudson Hotel, near Oka in Canada, was invaded by a poltergeist. Furniture leaped around, objects appeared and vanished and a fire broke out for no reason. The stable burned down and hotel guests were lucky to escape alive.

The haunted plains of Texas

▲A mighty stampede of phantom cattle has been known to appear over the Texas plains, and has even inspired a popular song, 'Ghost Riders in the Sky'.

The hauntings began in the 1870s when farmers began to settle in the Wild West. One of the cowboys who used to drive his cattle across the plains was so angry to find his route blocked by a farmer's house, that he drove the cattle straight through the farm. The cows began to stampede, crushing every living thing on the ranch.

It is said that screams of agony can still be heard as the phantom herd roars across the Texas sky.

▲A driver in New York State once gave a lift to two ghosts. He picked up an ordinary-looking couple hitch-hiking near a cemetery. When they reached Rochester, the driver turned to tell his passengers they had arrived—but they had vanished.

The Colorado ghost lights

▼The cemetery at Silver Cliff, Colorado, is haunted by weird, blue, glowing lights that hover above the graves at night.

They were first reported in the 1880s by miners working in the area, but these sightings were put down to drunkenness. However, the phantom lights kept appearing, even to sober people, and investigation proved they were real.

The mysterious lights became a tourist attraction after they were discussed in the *New York Times* in 1967. Some people still think they are a hoax, or a kind of reflection—but the Indians have long believed that the souls of the dead appear above graves as shimmering blue lights.

▲Another glowing ghost haunts a bridge in North Carolina, at the spot where a railway conductor was beheaded by a train. It is said that the flickering spectre is the man's body, searching for his head so that he can rest in peace.

▲A pirate who hid his treasure in his garden in Maryland, still guards it, although he has been dead for many years. He returns at full moon, turns into a blazing ball of fire and then rolls to the spot where his loot lies buried.

▲The bride of a New England widower woke in terror one night, as a ghost was pulling the rings from her finger. The mean farmer had taken the rings from the corpse of his first wife and her angry ghost had come to claim them back.

The Walsingham ghosts

In 1891, a house in Georgia, USA, became troubled by strange disturbances. Doors banged shut, bells rang and furniture moved about, all without any visible cause.

A farmer named Walsingham lived there with his family. At first they were not worried by the hauntings, believing that unfriendly neighbours or naughty children were to blame. However, as time went on, the Walsinghams began to believe in ghosts.

1. The hauntings seemed to begin when Mr Walsingham threw out some bones he found when they first moved in. The ghosts were quite invisible, but the whole family was kept awake at night by hideous screams and wails and terrible laughter.

2. It seemed that the Walsinghams' pets could see the spectres. The cat was stroked by invisible hands, but the dog always barked at the ghosts. When he attacked one, it threw him to the ground so hard his neck was broken.

3. The youngest daughter, saw a man's arm materialize one night. The ghostly hand rested on her shoulder. She could see it and feel it, but it did not reflect in the mirror she sat in front of. She screamed and the arm vanished.

4. One day, while walking in the garden, Mr Walsingham was accompanied by a spectre. He could not see it, but watched prints of a man's bare feet appear on the ground next to his own. It was as if the ghost was at his side.

5. The Walsinghams moved from the house after a dinner party was ruined. A loud groan was heard upstairs and blood began to drip from the ceiling onto the table. Nothing could be found in the room above to explain this horrific occurrence.

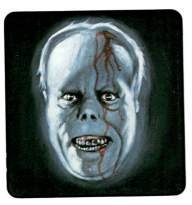

6. The empty house became an odd curiosity, until Horace Gunn spent a night there. He woke to see a human head, covered with blood, floating above his bed. It vanished, and Gunn ran from the room so terrified he could not scream.

7. In the hallway, he was grabbed around the throat by ice-cold, invisible hands and lay unconscious until the next day. Gunn never recovered from this night in the house, but afterwards the hauntings mysteriously stopped.

Australian apparitions

Australian hauntings, like those of America, tend to be very similar to the ghost stories of Europe. This is not surprising, as both countries were settled by Europeans, who took their own folklore traditions with them.

Many Australian apparitions seem to have been murder victims, who returned after death to pin the crime on the murderer and see justice done. An early example of this type of avenging ghost is the story of Fred Fisher, who vanished mysteriously in 1826. His ghost soon appeared, pointing to the ground. When this was dug up, Fisher's murdered body was found and his killer confessed to the crime.

▲In 1922 a phantom woman and child were seen near a beach in New South Wales, pointing at a cave. When it was searched two skeletons were found, along with papers that revealed the identity of a man who had murdered his wife and child.

▲In 1919 the headless ghost of a woman was seen hovering over a lagoon near Warpsarilla. When the sightings were investigated, a headless skeleton was discovered at the point where the spectre emerged from the mud. She too had been murdered.

Spectral evidence

◀A young policeman was riding through the Australian outback, when he saw a small, ghostly house suddenly appear out of nowhere. Two men ran out of the door. An old man, screaming with terror, was being chased by an evil-looking man brandishing an axe. The younger man then split open the skull of the other and the whole scene vanished.

The policeman stopped at the next house he came across and knocked at the door. He was shocked to find the door opened by the same man whose 'ghost' he had just seen wielding an axe. The murderer soon confessed to his crime.

Chinese ghosts

In China, evil spectres and spirits were known as 'Kuei'. They were thought to be the ghosts of people who had lived wickedly or died violently.

Kuei usually tried to harm the living and searched for victims to take their place in hell. But they had no powers over people who were brave and not afraid of them.

It was believed that plants, and even objects, had spirits that could leave their 'bodies' and haunt people. These were dangerous, but easily destroyed once they returned to their original forms.

▲A policeman named Yin saved a woman from being hanged by the ghost of a suicide. The spectre became angry and tried to kill Yin instead. They fought until dawn, when the ghost grew weak and turned into a piece of rotten wood.

▲A wise man named Ye spent a night at a haunted inn and was woken by four ghosts. The first was a woman who had hanged herself; the second, a murderer who had been beheaded. The third was a man who had burnt to death, and last was the yellow swollen form of a man who had died by drowning. As Ye was not afraid, the Kuei were powerless. He told them to stop haunting and to behave well, so that they might be rewarded with another life. The Kuei agreed, then vanished.

The haunted willow

1. When Lu Ch'ien bought a haunted house, he decided to get rid of the ghosts himself. One night he was woken by a letter being thrust through the window. It came from a spectre that called itself Commander Willow.

2. The message said that ghosts had lived in the house for a year and threatened to kill Lu if he stayed. A ghost suddenly appeared, but it vanished when Lu fired an arrow at it, leaving behind a gourd that it had been holding.

3. A few days later the spectre returned and Lu's servant shot at it. This time the ghost was hit in the chest and it ran off. Luckily, the ghost had left a trail of footprints showing which way it had gone.

4. Lu followed the footprints to the base of a huge willow tree, and found an arrow stuck in its trunk. The spectre had been a tree-spirit, and Lu chopped it down to burn as fuel in his now unhaunted house.

Funeral rites

Mourning and burial rites are often used to keep the souls of the dead from tormenting the living. In ancient times, people like the Egyptians were buried with ornaments and food to keep them contented in the after-life.

Spirits may be helped by prayer to get to heaven, or discouraged in various ways from staying on earth.

Mourning clothes were once worn as disguise, to confuse the souls of the dead, so ghosts could not haunt their living relatives.

▼In Ancient Egypt, corpses were made into mummies—completely dried and wrapped in bandages. As a mummy, the body was preserved so that the soul could return and live in the body in the next world.

The corpse was also buried with money, food pots and anything else it might need in the after-life.

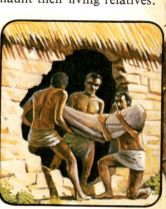

▲One way people have used to confuse ghosts was to take a corpse out of a house through a hole in a wall, rather than using the door. This was to stop the ghost finding its way back to haunt.

▲Some Australian aborigines used to bury their corpses within a ring of trees and cut a strip of bark from each. The ghost was then trapped in the circle that this created, not knowing which way to go. If a ghost was lost it could not haunt the living.

▶Mourners at funerals in many parts of the world sometimes disguised themselves by wearing special costumes. These were supposed to drive away evil spirits and prevent ghosts from recognizing them.

Some mourners wore rags and covered themselves with mud. This was to show the ghosts how terrible life on Earth was in the hope that they would go away and not haunt the living.

◀The head-hunters of New Guinea used the skulls of their dead relatives as pillows, in the belief that they warded off evil spirits.

They also used to eat parts of the corpse before the funeral, believing that this helped the soul pass on to the after-life.

The ghost of Marley
appears to Scrooge.

Ghosts in fiction

Often, when there is a haunting in literature, the ghosts have been used by the writer to make one of his characters think hard about his past life and feel guilty about what he has done.

One of the best known ghostly tales is 'A Christmas Carol', written in 1843 by Charles Dickens. This story tells how a mean old miser, Ebenezer Scrooge, is changed into a kind and charitable man by ghosts.

'A Christmas Carol'

The story begins one Christmas Eve. Scrooge is rude to a man collecting money for the poor and he is unpleasant to his nephew, who has invited him to a Christmas party. Scrooge does not enjoy Christmas and he complains because his clerk, Bob Cratchit, wants to take Christmas Day as a holiday to spend with his family.

The first ghost that appears is Marley, Scrooge's business partner who has been dead for seven years. At first, Scrooge does not believe his eyes and says that all ghosts are 'humbug', caused by indigestion. Marley has a warning for Scrooge. He explains that he is in dreadful torment because of the terrible things he did when he was alive. His soul cannot rest and he wears heavy chains and money boxes—the things he loved more than people before he died. He says that Scrooge will suffer the same fate, unless he reforms and that three ghosts will try to save him.

The next spirit is the Ghost of Christmas Past. The spectre takes Scrooge back in time to the happy Christmases he spent with his sister as a boy, and as a young man at parties, dancing and feasting. He sees how much he has changed over the years and begins to regret his mean actions. Soon Scrooge has a vision of a girl whom he would not marry because she was too poor. She is surrounded by her loving family and he feels very alone and miserable.

The next spirit is the Ghost of Christmas Present, who gives happiness to everyone who enjoys Christmas. He shows Scrooge how poor Bob Cratchit and his family are, yet how much they love each other and enjoy Christmas together. The youngest child, Tiny Tim, is crippled and the spirits warns that unless the future is somehow changed, this boy will die. The ghost shows Scrooge the many poor and sick people whom he makes happy every year at Christmas time.

The final spirit, the Ghost of Christmas Yet To Come, is the most frightening of all. He shows Scrooge his own death. At first Scrooge does not realize who it is people mourn so little. He sees the undertaker, the charlady and the washerwoman selling his clothes and even the blankets his corpse is wrapped in. Even kind people like Bob Cratchit and his nephew do not mourn him.

Scrooge wakes up from a deep sleep to find it is Christmas Day and he has a chance to put right some of the wrongs he has committed.

Driving out ghosts

Ghosts can be forcibly expelled. Evil spirits are usually driven off by a priest, who calls in the name of God in a ceremony called exorcism. There are also many ways used to repel or trap ghosts.

Usually, however, it is a suffering or frustrated spirit who returns from the dead, and it may be necessary to find out what troubles it. The spirit may be tied to Earth by its need for help, prayers, or (in many cases) a proper burial.

▲This is an old Welsh method of trapping ghosts. The exorcist conjured the ghost into a bottle and sealed it with a lighted candle. He told the ghost to stay there until the candle burned in water. Then he threw the bottle into a stream.

▲Among the Matumba people of central Africa, water was a weapon against ghosts. In one case a woman was thrown into a river to dislodge the spirit of her dead husband. He had clung to her back, refusing to depart to the spirit world.

▲The Algonquin Indians in Canada belived that the ghosts of their ancestors must be given offerings of food to keep them from haunting. One of their stories told of a man who was pushed into a fire by the ghost of a neglected ancestor.

▲The Angoni tribe of Zambia feared that the spirits of enemies they had killed could bring bad luck. After every battle the warriors ran through the village at daybreak, uttering frightful screams to drive away any lingering ghosts.

▲A haunting is sometimes a plea for help. The phantom priest shown here held a lonely service every year in a French chapel, until a brave man came to assist him in the service. Then the spirit seemed satisfied, and appeared no more.

▲Some ghosts are restless because their bodies are not buried. These may point out the place where their remains can be found and decently buried, or try to lead people there. When this is done, the soul is no longer earthbound, and departs.

▲Some Christians believe that ghosts are really demons, impersonating the spirits of the dead. In the ceremony of exorcism a priest casts out the demon in the name of God, using a prayer and holy water (water that has been blessed).

Investigating hauntings

During the 19th century, scientists studying how rocks are formed and biologists studying how animals lived often came up with theories that made religious ideas about the beginning of the world look mistaken. Some people in western Europe and America began to think that all the mysteries of the universe could be investigated, and hopefully explained, using scientific methods.

Though there have been ghost stories since the beginning of recorded history, it was not until the last half of the 19th century that people began to investigate reports of hauntings in a systematic way.

In 1890, the British Society for Psychical Research questioned 17,000 people to find out how many had actually seen a ghost. A total of 1,684 claimed that they had. Over half of them, 890, said that they recognized the ghost to be someone they knew.

Any investigation into ghosts ought to start with the collection of accurate information. On this page we show the kind of report form that could be used by any investigator who meets someone who claims to have seen or heard a ghost.

Ghost Report Form

1 Place......................
Date.......................
Time.......................

2 Appearance of ghost:
Shape......................
Size.......................
Colour.....................
Brightness.................
Transparancy...............
Behaviour of ghost:
Movement...................
Sounds.....................
Other......................

4 Any visible evidence ?.......
Any other strange occurances?
....

5 Sighting conditions:
Light......................
Weather....................
Were you looking for a ghost?
Are there reports of previous
hauntings here?............
Who saw the ghost?.........
Condition of witnesses.......
(health, eyesight, tiredness,
fright, cold, alertness.)

. . . .
. . . .
. . . .

3 Sketch ghost here.

. . . .
. . . .
. . . .

. . . .

. . . .

. . . .

. . . .

The ghost hunters

Perhaps the idea of someone being a ghost hunter is a little misleading. Most investigators spend their time interviewing people who claim to have seen ghosts. They try to discover if the reported hauntings are genuine, or whether there could be an ordinary explanation for the strange goings-on.

One of the most famous early researchers was Elliot O'Donnell. He believed that supernatural forces, both good and bad, were attracted to people interested in the subject. He investigated hundreds of weird hauntings from all over the world, and wrote many books about his experiences.

O'Donnell first saw a spectre when he was only five years old. Later on in life he was sure that he had seen a large number of spirits of many different types.

Harry Price, another ghost hunter, was also an expert on conjuring and magic. This helped him expose fake mediums who sometimes claimed they were able to make the spirits of the dead appear.

Although his most famous investigation was carried out at Borley Rectory, Price himself never saw a ghost in that most haunted of houses.

117

Fakes and mistakes

Ghost hunters and other researchers find it almost impossible to prove that a haunting is genuine, even if they are convinced themselves that it is. However, it is quite easy for them to expose the fakes and errors.

People often report having seen a ghost at night. In bad light, even an innocent pile of clothes can look like a horrible spectre. Eerie lights often turn out to be reflections from passing car headlights or nearby houses.

Many phantoms are really ordinary people. At night, on a lonely road, someone in dark trousers and hat and a pale coat may seem to be a floating, headless ghost.

Think twice before you say you have seen a ghost.

The vicar of Wapping

Many stories of hauntings come from people who believe a place is haunted just because they have been told that it is.

In 1971, a magazine about the occult published a story about a ghostly vicar who haunted the London docks at Wapping. The journalist who wrote the story soon received details of sightings from many people who lived in the area. Only the journalist knew the haunting was a hoax—as he had invented the phantom vicar of Wapping himself.

So many people claimed to have seen this non-existent ghost, that Colin Wilson, a psychical researcher, decided to conduct an experiment. He arranged for a hypnotist to make a woman believe that she would see the vicar at a certain time and place. Soon the woman reported back that she had seen the phantom vicar.

▲Smugglers sometimes invented stories of hauntings as a cover for their illegal activities. One gang, who hid smuggled brandy in Hadleigh Castle, England, started rumours of a spectral woman in white to keep away inquisitive locals.

▲In Japan, foxes were thought to possess supernatural powers. During World War II, the American army thought of making 'ghost' foxes, by covering live foxes with a glowing paint. They planned to release them to frighten the Japanese people.

Things that go bump in the night

Hundreds of hauntings are investigated each year by the Society for Psychical Research. In most cases it finds that the 'hauntings' have a natural, rather than a supernatural explanation.

Many of the hauntings occur in old houses and the phantom footsteps, groans and moans can often be traced to bad plumbing, or even to newly installed central heating.

All houses make creaking noises at night, because the drop in temperature makes the woodwork contract. If this happens to the floorboards it can sound just like footsteps.

Even the wind whistling in drain pipes may sound like a ghostly scream. Mysterious tapping noises usually turn out to be merely the dripping of rain or even taps. This may frighten some people and convince them that their house is haunted.

Rats and mice can also cause disturbances that sound like ghosts. If they run about in empty rooms, or inside walls, the sound of their scampering feet can be terrifying. Mice sometimes nibble through electrical wires and cause apparently unexplained fires, or even bell-ringing, like those investigated in Borley Rectory.

Phantom photographs

Towards the end of the 19th century, many photographers became interested in producing pictures of ghosts. Often photographers claimed they were trying to take ordinary pictures, and it was not until the print was developed that the 'ghost' showed up on the film.

Most spirit photographs have been proved to be fakes. Here we show you four ways to take your own ghost pictures, without having to stay up all night in a haunted house. Colour photographs are very difficult and expensive to fake, so we have used a black and white film for all the pictures here.

▲The picture above is the easiest kind of ghost photograph you can fake at home. First take a picture of an empty graveyard, or any spooky setting. Send the film to be processed, but ask to have the negatives back before they are made into prints. Paint a dark ghostly shape onto the negative. When it is printed, the 'ghost' will appear white.

▲Using a black and white 'instant picture' camera, take a picture of your 'ghost'. Keep the camera in exactly the same position and, before pulling the film out, take another picture without the 'ghost' person there. Anyone in the first picture, but not in the second will appear transparent in the final photograph. The phantom woman shown here is haunting the Tower of London.

The 'ghost' was dressed in black cloth and stood in front of a very dark brown blanket, in a dark room. The only light used came from an ordinary desk lamp.

▲Take a picture of someone dressed in light colours against a dark background. Press the 'rewind button' to stop the film moving forward and then take the background picture. When the film is developed, the dark parts of the first picture will disappear, leaving the light parts of the 'ghost' showing over the new background. This 'ghost' was really two people, each partly covered in black cloth.

▲To make this picture we used the two negatives shown above—one for the 'ghost' and one for the graveyard. The two negatives were taped one on top of the other. The final print is a mixture of the two negatives. Dress the ghost in dark colours. These show up clear on a negative, allowing details of the background to show through when they are printed.

Explanations?

Without doubt, many of the stories of haunted houses, phantom figures and ghostly apparitions can be traced back to the kind of fakes and mistakes mentioned on the previous four pages. After being thoroughly investigated, however, many of the mysteries remain unsolved.

People continue to believe in ghosts, even if they cannot explain them fully. There have been many attempts to explain ghosts. Here are some of the most common.

Souls of the dead

One popular idea is that ghosts are the souls of the dead. Many people think that human beings have a spirit or soul. During life the soul cannot be seen or heard apart from the body. At death, the soul is said to leave the body and go to another world. What happens to a soul after death is often thought to be connected with the way a person behaved when alive. The souls of good people are rewarded by going to heaven, those of bad people are punished by going to hell.

The souls that become ghosts are those that cannot go on to another world. Usually this is because they have not had a proper funeral ceremony.

The Devil in disguise

Some Christians believe that ghosts and poltergeists are one form that demons can take. They believe that these mysterious hauntings provide proof that evil exists as a power to challenge the goodness of Christ. These Christians believe in an after-life, but they do not think that ghosts are the souls of dead people. They believe they are apparitions used by a force opposed to Christ to deceive people into thinking there can be any life after death apart from with God.

Thoughts of the dying

It is possible that ghosts exist only in the mind's eye of the person who sees them. They may be visions produced as a result of telepathic signals sent from one mind to another.

This may be particularly true in cases where ghosts of the living appear to close friends or relatives just when someone is about to die. It seems likely that people in great danger, or dying, may be thinking about someone they love and long to see again. The telepathic explanation for ghosts suggests that if you think hard enough about someone you could create a sort of energy strong enough to send an image to the others person's mind.

Impressions from the past

The haunting ghosts which linger in one place for a long time and are spotted by many people over the years could also be explained as a sort of image created by energy.

Some people believe that all actions, especially violent ones, leave an impression on the place where they occurred. This can be picked up later by sensitive people who visit that place. They see the original event as if it were happening at that moment.

Testing explanations

A good explanation should help us understand why ghosts behave as they are said to. It might also help us to predict when ghosts are likely to appear. Here are some questions that a good explanation ought to be able to help us answer.
1. Why do ghosts appear so suddenly and then vanish?
2. Why are some people more likely than others to see ghosts?
3. How can a ghost know something a living person does not know?
4. Why do some ghosts warn people of danger?
5. How do the methods used for getting rid of ghosts really work?
6. Why are so many hauntings connected with sad events?

The first explanation, that ghosts are the souls of the dead, cannot answer any of the six questions unless we already believe that people have souls. Even if we believed this, we would still need more evidence to show that they can appear as ghosts.

Anyone who believes that ghosts are one form that demons can take, might also think that the devil has the power to make demons do anything he wishes in order to deceive people. For these people, therefore, this explanation might provide answers to all six questions. Unless we already believe that the devil exists, we have no way of testing whether or not the explanation is true.

The explanation that involves telepathy might explain ghosts of the living, but not those of the dead. Even so, we do not know how telepathy works.

The idea that violent actions can leave a mark on the air where they took place is exciting, but still there is no known means by which this could take place. In any case, if ghosts are impressions from the past, it is difficult to see how they could warn people of present or future danger or pass on news to the living.

All the explanations that have been discussed here share one thing in common. They all raise as many questions as they answer. If you believe you have a good explanation for hauntings, think hard about what it really says. Can it answer the kinds of questions listed above? Never accept an explanation unless you believe it would be possible to understand every part of it. It is better to admit that you do not understand something and go on searching for an answer, rather than to pretend you have an explanation for what is really a mystery.

Supernatural guide

In this section you will have read about many of the most well known stories of the supernatural world of ghosts and hauntings. On these pages we show some of the lesser known facts and ancient legends about hauntings.

ANKOU: This is the spirit of death that travels around the countryside of Brittany in northern France. He appears as a skeleton and pushes a creaky hand-cart. The Ankou's job is to collect the souls of the newly dead. The sight of the Ankou is a sign that a death is about to take place.

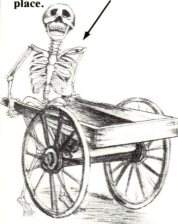

BANSHEE: A female spirit who heralds the death of members of certain Irish and Scottish families. Just before death, the banshee will begin to wail and scream in sorrow. According to one legend, a banshee appeared to a man of Irish descent predicting the death of President Kennedy in 1963.

BARGUEST: A phantom dog which brings death to all who see it. It is thought to be a large, shaggy black animal with eyes as big as saucers, most often found standing near churchyards. It has supernatural powers. Dogs like these have been reported in many parts of England and France.

DEATH SHIP OF WALCHERN: This phantom ship was believed by the Dutch to sail every autumn to carry the souls of the dead from Holland to England. This legend was supposed to explain why there were so many ghosts in England. The ship was steered by a white robed figure of death who had collected the spirits of the dead in Holland.

ELEMENTAL SPIRIT: This is the spirit of a natural object, like a tree or a stream. There were thought to be spirits of fire, air, earth, and water. Most elemental spirits were evil or, at least, very troublesome and harmful to humans. Earthquakes and mining accidents were blamed on earth spirits living underground. Some people still believe that poltergeist hauntings are caused by elementals.

FUNERAL WREATH: Some kind of floral offering has long been made to the dead. Funeral wreaths probably began as a 'magic circle' of flowers placed on a grave in the belief that it would stop the ghost returning. Offerings were also used as a mark of respect so the spirit would not feel angry and seek revenge.

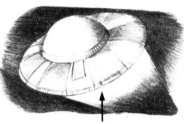

GHOSTS FROM THE FUTURE? Some people believe that ghosts are images that are mysteriously trapped in one place from another time. This theory is said to explain hauntings from the past—but it could also apply to Unidentified Flying Objects. Flying saucers could be ghosts from the future but we will not understand them until we reach the time in the future from which they have returned to haunt us.

TREASURE GUARDIAN GHOSTS: When pirates buried their treasure they often left someone behind to guard it. One pirate was murdered and his corpse buried with the loot. His ghost was thought to rise from the grave and frighten off anyone who tried to dig up the treasure and steal it.

HAUNTED TREES: In Nigeria, spirits of the dead were said to live in trees. The souls of all the Idem tribe were thought to live in one large tree. Anyone who harmed this tree was doomed to die.

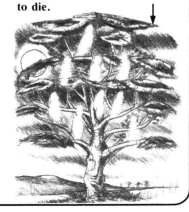

KING OF THE BROCKEN:
A giant ghost that, according to old legends, rules Mount Brocken in central Germany. The term 'Brocken-spectre' comes from these stories and is the name for apparitions seen in the sky by mountaineers. In fact these 'ghosts' are only the climbers' own shadows, cast on the clouds by the sun.

MEDIUM: Someone who claims to be in touch with the dead. Mediums sometimes go into a trance while passing messages between the dead and the living, during a seance (meeting).

OSIRIS: The ruler of the after-life in Egyptian mythology. Osiris was said to judge the souls of dead people to see if they were fit for life after death. If they were not, their hearts were eaten by a monster that was part hippopotamus, part crocodile and part lion.

PRETAS: These were the ghosts of Hindus, who had been very evil. They were also called the hungry ghosts, as they had such tiny mouths, they could not eat the offerings made to them. The Pretas suffered such terrible torment from this punishment, that they haunted the living to find bodies to steal and live in, so they could eat again.

REINCARNATION: The belief that a soul returns to earth after death, usually in a different body from the one it inhabited in its previous life.

SALT: According to Chinese legends, salt was very good for getting rid of ghosts. One story tells of how a man carrying salt, met a huge, black spectre on a country lane. He threw salt at the ghost and it vanished. The man returned to the lane next morning and found the salt all stained with blood. No ghosts were ever reported in that lane again.

SOUTER FELL: A hill in the English Lake District, where in 1735, a farm-hand saw a phantom army of marching troops. Two years later another army of spectral soldiers was seen marching, accompanied by a ghostly officer on horseback.

STYX: In Ancient Greek mythology the Styx was the river dividing the world of the living from Hades, the underworld, where dead souls went. In order to cross the Styx, the ferryman, Charon, had to be paid. This led to a custom of placing coins under the tongues of the dead, so they could get to Hades.

WANDERING GHOSTS: In China the ghosts of people whose bodies had not been buried, were said to cause drought. The homeless spirits cried and wailed in wet weather and tried to stop it raining, as they had no tomb or grave to shelter in.

WILD HUNT: A party of phantom huntsmen said to ride through the sky in autumn looking for living souls. On the eve of the French Revolution in 1789, peasants in the fields saw ghostly huntsmen in the air and their visit was interpreted as a sign of the coming trouble.

VERSAILLES: A Royal palace near Paris, the grounds of which are said to be haunted by ghosts of the 18th century royal court. The first report, in 1901, was thought to be an accidental sighting of a private historical drama, being acted out in the park. But the phantoms of people from the time of the French Revolution, have been seen a number of times during this century.

WRAITH: This is one name given to an apparition of a living person. It can be seen by others, although the person himself may not know that his wraith has left his own body.

Ghostly quiz

Now that you have read all about haunted houses, ghosts and spectres, test your knowledge by trying to answer these questions. The answers are at the bottom of the next page. They are printed upside down and back to front to make cheating more difficult. In order to read them, hold the page upside down in front of a mirror.

1 Which Scottish mountain does the Great Grey Man haunt?

2 Who haunts Dover Castle?

3 What did the Matumba people of central Africa use as a weapon against ghosts?

4 Which expert ghost hunter investigated the hauntings at Borley Rectory?

5 What were evil spirits and spectres called in China?

6 What is the name of the most haunted castle in France?

7 What haunts the Tay bridge?

8 Where is the ghost of Queen Elizabeth I sometimes seen?

9 Who stared in through the windows of Borley Rectory?

10 Where does a phantom woman without a tongue haunt?

11 Why did the Egyptians bury possessions, money and food with their dead?

12 Whose ghost warned King Charles I not to fight a battle on the next day?

13 What haunting inspired the popular song 'Ghost Riders in the Sky'?

14 Who wrote the ghost story 'A Christmas Carol'?

15 In which cemetery do weird blue lights hover above the graves at night?

16 Where did an invasion of mysterious hats occur?

17 What is the ghost of King George II said to mutter?

18 What sort of ghost haunts the crossroads at Echt in Holland?

19 Who sometimes invented tales of hauntings as a cover for their illegal activities?

20 What is the ghostly wild stallion which haunts the American prairies called?

21 Where can a human skull that is said to scream and bleed be found?

22 Who was often followed by a ghostly red figure?

23 Whose funeral train haunts the route it took through New York State, in 1865?

24 What is the name given to a phantom black dog, with eyes as big as saucers?

25 What does the ghost of a pirate who hid his treasure in a garden return as?

26 How many ghosts are said to haunt Glamis Castle?

27 Which tribe sleep on the skulls of dead relatives, to ward off evil spirits?

28 When does the phantom of the Lady Luvibond reappear?

29 What ghosts were seen over the plains of Marathon?

30 What shape do the ghosts of some drowned sailors take?

31. What did Harry Price find, when digging in the cellars of Borley Rectory?
32. Where have the phantom armies of King Charles I and Oliver Cromwell been seen?
33. In Ancient Greek mythology, which river divided the world of the living from Hades?
34. Which Everest expedition was haunted by a ghost climber?
35. What was the original meaning of the word 'poltergeist'?
36. What did the Algonquin Indians offer the ghosts of their dead ancestors?
37. Who was saved from a fatal lift crash by a ghost?
38. Where was a fake ghostly vicar said to be seen?
39. Which God judged the souls of the dead, according to Egyptian mythology?
40. What did Welsh exorcists use to trap ghosts?
41. What sort of ghost haunted Lu Ch'ien's house?
42. Where has President Abraham Lincoln's ghost been seen?

Answers

1. Ben Macdhui.
2. A headless drummer boy.
3. Water.
4. Harry Price.
5. King.
6. Chateau Blandy.
7. A phantom train.
8. Windsor Castle.
9. The phantom nun.
10. Glamis Castle.
11. To keep them content in the after-life.
12. The Earl of Strafford.
13. A stampede of phantom cattle over Texas.
14. Charles Dickens.
15. Silver Cliff, Colorado.
16. Killakee, Ireland.
17. 'Why don't they come?'
18. A headless woman.
19. Sunglasses.
20. The White Devil.
21. Borliscombe Manor, Dorset.
22. Napoleon Bonaparte.
23. Abraham Lincoln.
24. Bargeust.
25. A ball of fire.
26. Ten.
27. Head hunters of New Guinea.
28. Every 50 years on the anniversary of the Cunard sinking.
29. Greek and Persian soldiers.
30. Seagulls.
31. Part of a jawbone of a young woman.
32. Edgehill.
33. The Styx.
34. The Bonington expedition in 1975.
35. Noisy spirit in German.
36. Food.
37. Lord Duveen.
38. Wapping, London.
39. Osiris.
40. Bottles.
41. The ghost of a widow.
42. The White House.

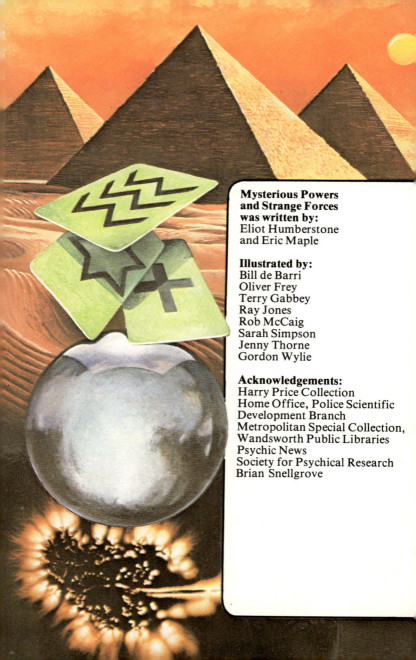

**Mysterious Powers
and Strange Forces
was written by:**
Eliot Humberstone
and Eric Maple

Illustrated by:
Bill de Barri
Oliver Frey
Terry Gabbey
Ray Jones
Rob McCaig
Sarah Simpson
Jenny Thorne
Gordon Wylie

Acknowledgements:
Harry Price Collection
Home Office, Police Scientific
Development Branch
Metropolitan Special Collection,
Wandsworth Public Libraries
Psychic News
Society for Psychical Research
Brian Snellgrove

Part 3

MYSTERIOUS POWERS & STRANGE FORCES

Introduction

People have long been aware of mysterious powers and strange forces. For thousands of years, reports have come from all parts of the world of people with unexplained abilities. Some were said to see into the future, or to float in the air. There are stories of others walking unharmed through burning fires or moving objects with the power of their thoughts.

This section describes many of these unexplained powers and phenomena. There are also some simple tests you can carry out to see if you can send messages with your mind and whether you can find hidden objects with the ancient art of dowsing.

Contents

Mysterious powers

There are people who can see and hear, not only with their eyes and ears, but also, so it seems, with their minds. For thousands of years there have been reports of people who have the power to see into the future. Some have dreams which later come true, some see visions in crystal balls, while others read the future in the tea leaves at the bottom of a cup.

In the past, many of the people who have demonstrated these mysterious powers have been condemned as witches or wizards. Others have been respected as wise and holy men.

Many quite ordinary people have had experiences that have made them think that there are other ways of finding out about the world apart from their normal senses of touch, sight, hearing, smell and taste. They, like the holy men and the witches, have what is known as 'extra-sensory perception', ESP.

The main forms of ESP are clairvoyance, telepathy and precognition. Clairvoyance is the power of finding out about something, using only the mind and none of the ordinary senses. For instance, some people, if given a sealed envelope with a message inside, can sense what the message is without opening the envelope. Telepathy is the ability to read another person's mind and precognition is the strange power of knowing the future before it happens.

However they work, these mysterious powers challenge all our ordinary ways of thinking about the world. The same is true of the amazing powers some people seem to possess to bend metal or move objects by the energy of their thoughts alone. The physical world, it seems, and the laws of nature, can be influenced by people's minds.

Some people, it appears, can vanish in one place, only to reappear the next moment somewhere completely different. Some of the most ancient legends in the world tell of holy men in India and Tibet who can lift themselves up into the air. If men can defy gravity and learn to fly, there is perhaps no limit to the things we can do, if the secrets of these mysterious powers can be set free.

133

Premonitions of disaster

People sometimes have the feeling that they know something is going to happen. This is called a premonition. Some premonitions take the form of dreams or visions. Others are just strong feelings, ideas or guesses that come into people's minds for no apparent reason.

Most people think that they have premonitions at one time or another, but some people, known as 'psychics' appear to be more sensitive to whatever causes accurate premonitions.

Many premonitions are about death and disaster. The story here about the tragic disaster of the Titanic and the many mysterious forewarnings that were reported.

The sinking of the Titanic

In the early morning of April 15, 1912, the Titanic, the world's largest ocean liner at the time, struck an iceberg and sank on her maiden voyage across the Atlantic. A total of 1,502 lives were lost. Later investigation turned up at least 20 cases of people having premonitions of the disaster.

One of the strangest examples of an apparent

premonition involved a novel called 'Futility', written in 1898 by Morgan Robertson. In the book, a huge liner, the 'Titan', sank after hitting an iceberg. Like the Titanic, the Titan was said to be unsinkable. Also like the Titanic, the Titan carried too few lifeboats for the large number of passengers on board.

As well as this, there were two other stories that appeared to foretell the disaster, both written by a passenger on the doomed ship—one of them over 20 years earlier.

At least nine people had dreams in which a ship like the Titanic hit an iceberg and sank. Two clairvoyants gave warnings about the disaster and several other people had strangely strong intuitions that something would go wrong. Some would-be passengers were so uneasy about the voyage that they cancelled their tickets at the last minute. All these uncanny coincidences appear to be premonitions. In any case, there seems to be no way of explaining them.

Crystal gazing

Not all premonitions are unexpected. Some people seem to be able to look into the future whenever they want to. These people are called 'seers'. Almost all of them use something to encourage visions to appear in their minds. Seer's aids help them to relax and concentrate so their minds are receptive to images of the future.

One of the most usual aids, is a crystal ball. Seers can also see into the past life of people who consult them. By gazing into a crystal ball the seer focuses his mind. After a few minutes he might see a vision of the future or the past in the crystal ball. Sometimes he can even see the whereabouts of a lost object in a crystal ball vision.

Today most seers use a solid glass ball. In the past polished rock crystal, like that below, was used.

▲ In 1876 a young French man called Bertaux had his fortune told by a gypsy at a fairground. She said that he would become head of the army but saw a vision of his death in her crystal ball; he would be killed by a 'flying chariot.'

Bertaux was suprised by her predictions as he did not

▲ Almost any shiny surface can help a fortune teller to have visions of the future. Bowls of water and mirrors were often used in Europe, but seers in Ancient Egypt gazed into pools of blood.

▲ In parts of North Africa people used to smear their thumbnails with soot and oil to produce a dark glistening surface to stare into while trying to see the future.

want a military career and aeroplanes did not yet exist. However, he became a politician and was made Minister of War—head of the army. In 1907, while attending a display of the new military aircraft, Bertaux was killed, when one of the planes crashed into the crowd.

▲ Psychic priests of the Huron Indians of Canada used the dark silky fur of squirrels to encourage their prophetic visions. They also used to stare into the shiny glaze on china, or into pools and bowls of water.

Signs of the future

Some seers do not have direct visions of the future. Instead, they interpret ordinary chance events, like the way dice fall or the way cards are dealt after being taken from a well shuffled pack. This sort of fortune-telling is called divination. It includes reading the patterns that are made by tea leaves at the bottom of a cup and interpreting patterns in sand or wheat after it has been scattered on the ground. It is usually thought that some people are better than others at reading the signs.

Sometimes a method of divination has been used for only one sort of question about the future. Many tribes that relied on hunting animals for food used to throw bones on the ground to find where the best hunting grounds were. These bones were like an early form of modern dice. The pattern the bones made would show them where to go hunting.

Because the bones made a different pattern each time they were thrown, no one part of the hunting ground was ever overhunted. This could explain why an apparently mysterious method of divination may have been successful.

The Tarot cards

▼ Diving the future from the symbols on playing cards dealt to someone, is called cartomancy. It has been popular in Europe since the 14th century, when cards were thought to have been introduced by gypsies from India.

The earliest type of cards were Tarot cards, which were probably designed as a way of fortune-telling. Each Tarot card has a picture with a special meaning for the person whose fortune is being told. This is known only by the diviner, dealing the cards. Those shown below are called Death, the Final Judgement, The Tower, The Sun and The Devil.

Ancient omens

▲ According to one legend, a Roman emperor cut short a journey because he believed the flight pattern of some eagles to be a bad omen. The following night, the room in which he would have slept is said to have collapsed.

People have interpreted many different things as signs of the future. They have even 'read' the intestines of animals.

In one ancient form of divination, known as 'daphnomancy', the branches of a bay tree were set on fire. If they crackled loudly in the flames this was supposed to be a very good omen for the future.

139

Prophecy and visions

Many people have had sudden visions of the future and some have become famous for their prophecies.

These predictions are more likely to be remembered if they come true, than if they are mistaken. Most prophets express their ideas about what will happen in the future in a very vague way. Because of this, people are able to interpret them in whichever way seems best.

England's best known prophet was Mother Shipton. Many of her predictions seem to have been accurate.

▲ In 1888 the future came to a Canadian man in the form of a huge black monster with one dazzling eye in the centre of its head. Only 25 years later did he realize what it was, when a railway was built through the place where he saw his vision.

▲ In 1788 a French seer named Jaques Cazotte made several prophecies at a dinner party, all of which came true. He even foresaw his own death on the guillotine. The following year he was executed during the French Revolution.

▲ Pope Pius V is said to have had a vision of the Christians' naval victory over the Turks at Lepanto on the day it took place. The Pope was in Rome at the time and news confirming his vision did not arrive until two weeks later.

Mother Shipton

▲ Mother Shipton, said to be the daughter of a witch, was born in Yorkshire in 1488. Many of her prophecies came true during her lifetime. However, some have only recently been understood, as they apparently refer to very modern inventions.

▲ Mother Shipton usually wrote her predictions as short rhyming verses. She correctly prophesied that the Great Fire of London would devastate the city and that the steeple of St Paul's Cathedral would be destroyed in an earlier fire.

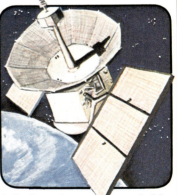

▲ Submarines were not invented until the 1880s, yet Mother Shipton prophesied 'Under water men shall walk, shall ride, shall sleep, shall talk'. She also foresaw iron ships which were not invented until several centuries after her death.

▲ Perhaps her most remarkable prophecy was 'Around the world words shall fly in the twinkling of an eye'. This has been said to have been fulfilled in the past century, with the invention of the telegraph, telephone, radio and television.

Mysterious dreams

Dreams have always been a mystery. People once thought that a soul could leave the body of a dreaming person. Scientists still cannot explain exactly what happens when we dream. It is now thought that every night we all spend about a third of our sleeping time having dreams, even if we do not remember them the next morning.

Some dreams bring knowledge of the real world to people while they sleep and these are the most commonly reported type of extra-sensory perception.

▲ According to the Bible, a king of Egypt dreamed that seven thin cows ate seven fat cows. A prophet then foretold, apparently correctly, that this meant that Egypt would have seven years of plenty, followed by seven years of famine.

Night of mourning

When he was a child, Abraham Lincoln dreamed that he would become a world famous figure.

Early in 1865, President Lincoln dreamed about his own death. In the dream he heard the sound of weeping in the White House. He went to the East Room of the White House and found a corpse lying in state, surrounded by mourners. Lincoln asked who was dead. A guard replied, 'It is the president, he was killed by an assassin'.

In April 1865, Abraham Lincoln was shot dead while at the theatre in Washington. His body was laid in state in the East Room of the White House.

Nightmare news

At about eight o'clock one night in August 1883, Edward Samson, a writer on a newspaper in Boston, USA, fell asleep in his office. At three o'clock the next morning he woke after a terrible nightmare. He had been dreaming of crowds of people rushing towards the sea, trying to escape an ocean of boiling lava. He saw ships crushed beneath huge waves and then a volcanic explosion which destroyed an entire island. Men and women screamed as they tried to escape being buried alive in the lava.

The dream was so vivid that Samson decided to write it down on some paper which he left on his desk. The next day his editor picked up the story and, thinking that it was an account of a real news story, published it in the paper. Samson had to explain that it had only been a dream.

Within days, however, a genuine news story came through about an island near Java in the Pacific Ocean. During the night of Samson's dream, the volcanic island of Krakatoa had blown up. Over 36,000 people had died and dozens of ships had been sunk in a tidal wave. The sun and moon appeared blue and vivid sunsets, caused by volcanic ash floating in the air were seen as far away as London.

Hypnotism

Some people have the power to put other people into trances. This is called 'hypnotism'. A hypnotized person is not in full control of his thoughts and actions. The hypnotist can easily persuade him to do many things he would not ordinarily do, such as act like a dog. However, it is impossible to make someone who is in a trance do something which they are strongly opposed to, such as commit murder or theft.

Hypnotists can also persuade people to follow their suggestion, even after the trance is ended. This is known as 'post−hypnotic suggestion'.

Hypnotism has many uses and some doctors and dentists use it to stop people feeling any pain during minor operations. It can also help people give up dangerous habits such as smoking cigarettes.

▶ Most people can be put into a hypnotic trance, but some are easier to hypnotize than others. Trances vary from very deep to fairly light, according to the subject's state of mind and the ability of the hypnotist. Many hypnotists use a bright light, a swinging pendulum or a rythmic sound to focus the subject's attention. They then 'talk' them into a trance. It is best to wake subjects slowly, by counting from ten to zero and suggesting they will wake a little upon hearing each number.

◀ In a deep hypnotic trance, the subject's body often becomes rigid. It is possible to balance someone in a trance across two chairs, supported only at the neck and feet, and even to place a heavy weight on his body. This would not be possible if the person were not hypnotized.

Hypnotists can sometimes make people experience hallucinations. A group of people was once told that they would see a square circle. Afterwards they said they did see it but found it impossible to describe.

Hypnosis and ESP

Some psychical researchers think that people's ESP powers increase when they are under hypnosis. Experiments to test subject's abilities to see the future and receive messages by telepathy, while in a trance, have been quite successful.

One Russian investigator, Professor Leonid Vasilyev, did a great deal of research into hypnosis and ESP during the 1920s and 30s. He found that he could put some people into a trance simply by thinking hard. This power was very strong and even worked over long distances. In one case, Vasilyev hypnotized someone who was over 1000km away.

Hypnotic traveller

A French psychologist named Professor Janet, was able to send a hypnotized patient on a psychic journey. He told the girl to travel with her mind to see what his friend Professor Richet was doing in Paris—over 190 km away from Le Havre, where they were at the time.

She suddenly shouted, 'It's burning, I tell you it's burning' and described how a fire was raging in Richet's laboratory. Richet later confirmed the girl's account of this fire which had gutted his laboratory at the exact time of Professor Janet's strange experiment.

Remembering past lives?

During the 1950s, a hypnotist named Arnall Bloxham found what some people believe to be proof that one person may have more than one life.

Bloxham hypnotized a man and then asked him to think back in time to a past life. Soon the man in a trance began talking about life in the 17th century. Bloxham hypnotized other people, many of whom told vivid stories from history which they could not have known about through any ordinary means.

▲ One woman, called Jane Evans, 'remembered' being a Roman in 3rd century York. All the details of her story fitted in with what historians know to be true, though Jane knew very little history.

▲ Graham Huxtable does not believe that people live more than one life, although under hypnosis he talked about life as a sailor in the early 19th century. He even screamed with pain as he told of being wounded in the leg at a battle. Huxtable thought that he could have inherited his accurate knowledge of life on a British warship from one of his ancestors, who may have been a sailor.

Journey through time

While hypnotized by
Bloxham, Jane Evans also
seems to have 'remembered'
at least five lives apart from
her time in 3rd century York.

She lived in York once
again in the 12th century. She
lived in the Loire Valley in
France in the 15th century.
Mrs. Evans also remembered
life in 16th century Spain,
17th century England and
recalled being a nun in the
USA at the beginning of the
20th century.

Perhaps her most terrifying
memory was an incident from
her life in 12th century York.
Jane Evans said she was a
women called Rebecca who
was being persecuted because
she was Jewish. She told of
how she was chased by an
angry anti-Jewish mob and
described how the Christians
burned down the castle where
some Jews were hiding. She
and her family escaped and
hid in the safety of a small
church crypt.

At the time Mrs Evans told
her story, no one knew of
any 12th century church
fitting her description that
also had a crypt. Sometime
afterwards, her story was
confirmed when workmen
digging beneath a 12th
century church discovered a
crypt. 'Rebecca' appears to
have known things which
Jane Evans could not have
known.

Trances

Some people can put themselves into trances. These are states of mind in which a person may become aware of things which he can not ordinarily sense. A person in a trance may also be able to shut out feelings he does not want. A trance is similar to the state of mind produced by a hypnotist, except that someone in a trance usually learns how to control this state himself.

People can go into trances as a result of meditation or prayer, wild dancing or eating special plants. All these methods can, however, be very dangerous. Often only priests or medicine men go into trances.

In some trances, if a person believes fire will not hurt him, then he will not be burned. This power of the mind over reality has never been properly explained.

Many religious people who go into trances believe that they can see or speak with God. Other people have thought that in a trance they can magically visit the future or the past—although their bodies remained where they were.

Most forms of trance are said to be pleasant, but sometimes a trance is like a spell of madness and can be terrifying for a person who fears he will never return to his normal state of mind.

▲ Many of the medicine men of the North American Indians used trances as a way of seeing the future. The Ojibway tribe built special wigwams, which shook violently and produced showers of sparks while the medicine man was inside in a trance.

▲ Among some Lapp tribes, the medicine man used to go into a trance while someone beat the magic drum which he wore on his back. The Lapps say his soul flies off to the spirit world, where it gets news of the future from gods and dead ancestors.

▲ People can become immune to pain while in a state of trance. Some even manage to walk through blazing fires or across hot coal without suffering ill effects. Although the fire is real and hot, it does not even burn the fire-walker's flesh or clothes.

▲ Some Indian 'fakirs' can rest on a bed of nails without feeling any pain or puncturing their skin while in a trance. Their muscles become hard and rigid and they can also control their breathing and heartbeat, which people cannot normally do.

Indian rope trick

The Indian rope trick is perhaps an example of mass hypnosis. People see a boy climb up an unsupported rope and vanish at the top. They see something that is not really happening, although they believe it is and so see it.

One man who saw this trick was surprised to find that on a photograph he had taken the rope lay coiled on the floor, with the boy standing next to it. This is not what he thought he had seen.

149

Battlefield visions

Mysterious visions of phantom armies have been seen on old battlefields all over the world. As recently as 1956, two men saw a phantom army rushing across the Isle of Skye, off north-west Scotland.

Strange visions have also been reported by soldiers fighting at war. These could simply be hallucinations caused by the stress and fear of battle, or even mistaken sightings of real people.

The angels of Mons

Some extraordinary reports of phantom soldiers occurred at the beginning of World War I. On September 29th, 1914, just after the British retreat from the battle of Mons, a London newspaper published a story by Arthur Machen, called 'The Bowmen'. In this story, Machen imagined St George sending a band of ghostly archers to help save the British army. Just at the time 'The Bowmen' was published, British soldiers fighting in Belgium began reporting strange visions—including the sight of St George. On the night of August 27th, a senior officer said he had seen squadrons of cavalry riding across the fields accompanying British soldiers on their way back from the front. This vision lasted for over 20 minutes and was shared by two other officers. British soldiers were not the only ones to see weird figures. French troops around the battlefields of Mons and Ypres saw apparitions of St Michael and Joan of Arc.

In 1930 a former chief of German espionage claimed that German pilots had shone pictures of angels onto the clouds. They thought that this would make the enemy believe that God was on the side of the Kaiser. Even if this explains the angelic figures seen near Mons, it leaves open the mystery of the squadrons of cavalry and the sight of St George.

▼ A vision of St George, the patron saint of England, was seen by many British soldiers. He appeared out of a cloud of light, wearing medieval armour, and charged across the sky as if riding to the rescue.

▲ The day after 'The Bowmen' was published, one soldier said he had seen three angelic figures wearing shining robes in the night sky, while he was retreating from Mons. His vision lasted 35 minutes.

Astral travelling

Some people seem to go through a strange experience called astral travelling, where their mind becomes separated from their body. This is also known as an 'out-of-the-body experience' or 'OOBE' for short.

During astral travel a person sees his own body as if it were another person. His mind seems to have moved into an 'astral body'. OOBEs are generally said to be pleasant experiences—although rather strange.

The astral traveller is not,bound by the limits of his physical body, so can travel to a place as fast as he thinks of doing so. The astral body can also pass through solid objects like walls and doors. Some people believe that the astral body is a person's soul.

Most OOBEs are accidental. They occur when a person is under stress, such as in a car crash or during a severe illness. However, some people seem to have the power to astral travel at will, whenever they want.

Leaving the body

Many people go through an out-of-the-body experience when they are very tired and just about to drop off to sleep. It might begin with the person seeing his body lying on the bed and having the feeling that he is floating above it.

The astral traveller may start to imagine what it is like to move in his spirit body. Sometimes he will find he is able to pass through physical objects and float off wherever he wants to go.

At first, the astral body hovers above the physical body.

According to many reports, the astral traveller is attached to his physical body by a silver cord that links the two heads.

Looking at Mercury

Ingo Swann, a painter from New York, can project his mind to anywhere on Earth and even to Outer Space. He calls this strange ability, which in some ways is like astral travelling, 'remote viewing'. Swann relaxes in a comfortable chair and concentrates on wherever he has been asked to visit.

In 1974, two weeks before the American spacecraft Mariner 10 visited Mercury, Swann sent his mind on a remote viewing test to the unknown planet. Reports later sent back from Mariner 10 confirmed some of what Swann 'saw'. He had said, accurately as it turned out, that Mercury's atmosphere was very thin and that there was a beautiful aura around the planet.

After gently leaving the body, the astral traveller can stand upright. But first he feels himself swaying to and fro.

Sometimes the astral body is visible to other people. It can look either pale and ghostly, or it can look like the real person.

Psychic voyage

Many out-of-the-body experiences appear to happen in order to save the life of the astral traveller. At times of great pain, people sometimes feel as if they are apart from their bodies. This helps them to stop feeling pain, so they can cope with the dangerous situation.

Sometimes, though not often, astral bodies can be seen by others. The story here was reported by a ship's captain in the 1860s. It involves something that appears to be very like astral travelling. In this case the traveller's only knowledge of his journey came in the form of a dream.

1 Robert Bruce, first mate of the ship, went below deck to the captain's cabin and found an odd stranger standing at the desk, writing in the log book. Bruce was terrified as no-one could have boarded the ship since they left Liverpool.

2 Bruce rushed up to the deck to tell the captain. When he reported what he had seen, the captain refused to believe it. The story seemed impossible, but when they looked at the log book they saw written in it, 'Steer to the Nor'west'.

3 The captain suspected a joke and decided to find out who had written the words. He tested the whole crew by asking them all to write 'Steer to the Nor'west'. Not one of them had handwriting like that which had mysteriously appeared in the log book.

4 Robert Bruce was sure that he had seen the man, although there was no sign of him aboard. The captain was puzzled and decided to follow the directions of the strange message. Three hours later they discovered a ship stuck in the frozen sea.

5 The crew went out in boats to fetch the survivors, who had almost given up hope of being saved. Bruce was shocked to find that he recognized one of the rescued sailors—it was the man he had seen in the captain's cabin, writing in the log book.

6 When the captain tested the man's handwriting, everyone was suprised to see that it matched the mysterious original. Robert Bruce explained what he had seen a few hours before, down in the captain's cabin. The stranger could not remember writing the message, but recalled that he had fallen into a deep sleep at about that time. He had vividly dreamed that he was on board a ship which was coming to save them. He even described this ship; it was identical to the real rescue vessel.

Doubles

Some people have had the uncanny experience of seeing themselves. It is as if people have two bodies—and it is their 'psychic double' also known as a 'doppelganger' which they see.

One explanation for the appearance of such a second self, is that it is a person's astral body. In most cases of astral travelling the mind of the person goes with the astral body while the normal body sleeps. It could be that sometimes the astral body separates from the physical body during a normal waking state, unnoticed.

▼ The German poet Goethe saw his double in 1771. He was riding home from visiting a friend when he noticed a man on horseback coming towards him. Suddenly Goethe saw that it was himself. However the figure was wearing a grey suit with gold trimmings, unlike anything he

◀ Seeing your own psychic body has long been thought of as a very bad omen—a sign of impending doom, often death. Sometimes doubles have been able to give a warning about the future to their 'real selves'.

Perhaps the astral body exists in a different time scale and is able to see what is going to happen, before it actually occurs to the physical body.

In 1822, the poet Shelley had a warning of his early death at the age of 30. He was living in Italy, in a house close to the sea when he saw his double. The double appeared on the terrace of the house, turned and pointed out towards the sea. It suddenly vanished as mysteriously as it had arrived. Within a few weeks Shelley's corpse was washed up on the beach. He had drowned in a boating accident, at sea.

possessed. The vision then disappeared. Eight years later, while riding along the same path, Goethe recalled the incident. He was shocked to realize that he was dressed in the same clothes that his double had been wearing. Had Goethe had a glimpse into his own future?

157

Mind over matter

The ability to move objects by the power of thought alone is known as psychokinesis, or 'PK' for short. It is a force that has never been properly explained, although it is the subject of many scientific tests. An American scientist, J. B. Rhine, began investigating PK in the 1930s. He set up experiments using dice, to see if people could cause them, by will power alone, to fall with a particular face uppermost. Many subjects seemed able to produce the desired results more often than was likely by chance alone.

One Russian woman, called Madame Kulagina, appears to possess PK powers strong enough to lift small objects, such as matchsticks, into the air. When she concentrates in a PK experiment, her heart beats 240 times per minute-over three times faster than normal. Her brain waves show that she is under stress and she sometimes loses as much as 1kg in weight.

Some people believe that PK may be an explanation for poltergeist activity. If objects fly about a room with no reason, someone may have PK powers without knowing it.

'Thoughtography'

The two pictures on the left, show an example of the 'thought photographs' made by a Chicago man, Ted Serios, during PK tests in the 1960s.

Serios concentrated hard on the church, shown in the top picture, while staring onto the lens of a camera. After a while he yelled to his assistant to snap the shutter. When the film was processed, he had created a result like the lower picture.

Neither Ted Serios, nor the scientists who have tested him, have any explanation of how the power of thought is able to affect photographic film.

Uri Geller

An Israeli psychic, named Uri Geller, has become world famous for his PK abilities. He is best known for bending metal forks and spoons, either by stroking them gently or else without touching them at all.

Geller often appears on television to demonstrate his powers and when he does, he asks viewers to check their own cutlery. On many occasions people watching Geller on television have reported that forks and spoons have bent even if they were not touching them. Clocks, watches and electrical gadgets of all kinds that were broken, have mysteriously started to work again during the psychic's television appearances.

For some mysterious reason, bending forks and spoons with psychic energy was unknown before Geller. Since 1970 several other people, including young children, have claimed they share Geller's powers.

Geller is a showman who has often performed on stage for money. Stage magicians have claimed that some of Geller's strange effects could be convincingly produced by conjuring. This is why some people are reluctant to agree that Geller's powers are genuine. Nevertheless, many people, including scientists, have been convinced after studying Geller, that his ESP and PK powers are real.

Levitation

Some people seem to have the ability to defy the power of gravity and rise up into the air. This is called levitation. Most reports of people levitating, describe them as hovering a few feet above the ground, although occasionally the levitators are said to move through the air, as if flying.

Over 200 saints of the Roman Catholic Church are supposed to have levitated, sometimes without warning and sometimes deliberately. Spiritualists—people who believe it is possible to communicate with the dead—as well as Hindu mystics, have claimed that levitation is possible during certain kinds of trances.

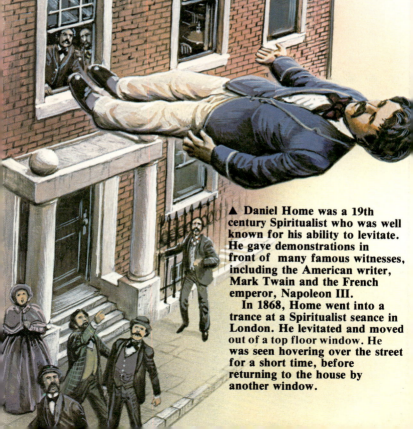

▲ Daniel Home was a 19th century Spiritualist who was well known for his ability to levitate. He gave demonstrations in front of many famous witnesses, including the American writer, Mark Twain and the French emperor, Napoleon III.

In 1868, Home went into a trance at a Spiritualist seance in London. He levitated and moved out of a top floor window. He was seen hovering over the street for a short time, before returning to the house by another window.

The flying monk

St Joseph of Copertino was one of the many Catholic saints who is said to have levitated. Giuseppe Desa, as he was originally called, was a young monk in northern Italy in the 17th century. He became known for his kindness, his holiness—and his ability to levitate.

In about 1625 he began to rise into the air while saying his prayers. Without being able to stop himself, he once rose into the air during a religious service. He was soon asked to say his prayers in private, as his sudden flights disturbed the other monks.

On another occasion, Giuseppe flew up and perched on the branches of an olive tree. It seemed as if he had become as light as a bird, because his weight did not break the branches.

Floating on faith

Earlier this century, a man travelling in Tibet came to a deep valley he wanted to cross. Suddenly he found he and his luggage had been carried up and across to the other side of the chasm. Most cases of levitation however, have little practical value. Levitation usually takes place while someone is saying prayers, meditating or as a result of a magical ritual.

In Europe levitators were sometimes accused of being witches. In Asia levitation was more often a sign that someone was very holy. It was said to be a power that could be learned through spiritual devotion and discipline. There have been many reports from India of holy men who could float in the air, or even over water, while they meditated.

Teleportation

Teleportation is the act of moving from one place to another without travelling through any of the places in between. Teleportation is a rare phenomenon, usually said to involve suddenly vanishing in one place, only to reappear the next moment somewhere completely different.

One of Uri Geller's friends, who is also a psychical researcher, claims that Geller has appeared on at least eight different occasions. He was once said to have teleported himself nearly 60km for a brief visit to his friend in New York, USA.

▲ It is said that the Spanish nun, Sister Mary of Agreda, teleported herself to America over 500 times in the 17th century. The Indians of New Mexico claimed to have been converted by her and even had a chalice from her convent.

Across the Pacific

In October 1593, a soldier suddenly appeared out of thin air, in front of the Palace in Mexico City. He looked confused and did not seem to know where he was. When arrested, the soldier claimed that his orders that morning had been to guard the palace in Manila, a city in the Philippines.

He realized that he was not there now but had no idea at all how he got to Mexico City. The last thing he could remember was that the palace had been overrun and the governor murdered.

The soldier was thrown into jail but two months after his strange journey, a ship arrived from the Philippines, bringing news of the governor's death, which confirmed his story.

The lost kilometres

Ray Stanford is an American psychic who claims he has been teleported three times. Stanford's first instant journey though it was only a short one, may have saved his life. In 1971, Stanford was galloping on a horse through some woods when he saw he was about to have his head knocked off by an overhanging branch. The next moment, Stanford found himself standing still about six metres from his horse. He had not been thrown and he could discover no footprints in the muddy ground that might have explained how he came to be where he was.

On another occasion, Stanford was in a queue of traffic on a Texas road. He realized that the lorry in front of him was dangerously close, so he slammed on the brakes and the next thing he knew, he was seven cars ahead in the stream of traffic. Although his car was ruined as he crashed down, Stanford's life had been saved.

Some time later, Stanford and his wife were again travelling along this stretch of road. They were hurrying to meet Uri Geller at Austin Airport when they began to think how useful it would be if they could teleport themselves towards their destination.

Suddenly the scenery changed. Ray Stanford, his wife and their car had been teleported to a spot nearly 60km closer to Austin. In their mysterious journey the Stanfords had averaged 200kph, although the maximum speed possible in the traffic conditions was only 100kph. At the end of the day Stanford inspected the car. It had used an enormous amount of fuel and all the electrical systems appeared charred. It looked as if the wires had been burned by whatever force it was that had carried them instantly over the kilometres.

Photographs of energy?

In 1939, Semyon Kirlian, a Russian electrician, found a way of taking pictures without using light or even a camera. He accidently put his hand and some film in the path of an electric current passing between two electrodes.

When the film was developed, a glowing image of his hand appeared. It was surrounded by bright shining dots and streams of coloured light.

Kirlian pictures seem to show that all living things and some inanimate objects have a twinkling aura that constantly surrounds them. It could be that these Kirlian 'photographs' show natural electrical energies.

▲Non-living objects usually show a steady unchanging aura on Kirlian photographs. However, things with a personal meaning, like the cross shown above, that are worn next to someone's body, often reflect the mental state and aura of their owner.

▲This Kirlian photograph of a leaf was taken after the top had been cut off. It shows the aura glowing around the missing part as if it were still there. The plumes of light vary according to the health of the leaf. They are strongest when it is first picked, but fade away as the leaf slowly dies and the mysterious energy leaves it.

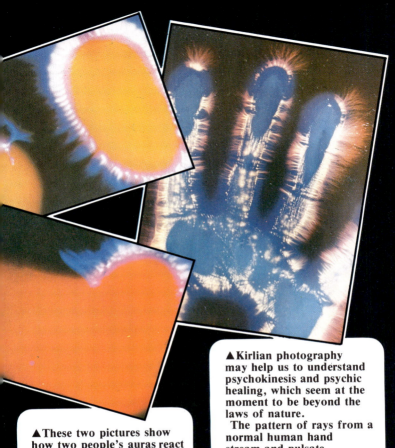

▲These two pictures show how two people's auras react to each other. The top photo is of two people's fingertips, placed side by side. The two are having unpleasant thoughts about each other. The auras do not touch, and even draw back from each other. The lower photograph shows what happens when the two people kiss—their auras flow towards each other and mingle together.

▲Kirlian photography may help us to understand psychokinesis and psychic healing, which seem at the moment to be beyond the laws of nature.

The pattern of rays from a normal human hand stream and pulsate, changing colour often, according to the thoughts and emotions of the subject. Diseases seem to show up in Kirlian photographs as a distorted aura before any other symptoms become visible.

Some psychic healers produce large, strong auras, which stream out towards the patient during healing sessions.

Can plants feel?

Plants were often worshipped by ancient peoples because it was believed they possessed magical properties and powers. Plants, especially trees, were said to have some sort of soul.

Today most people think of plants as living, but quite unconscious things, having no feelings or emotional response to the world around them.

However, in 1966, in the USA, experiments on plants began which, suggest to some people that plants not only feel, but may also have highly developed extra- sensory perception.

Testing plant growth

Some experiments have suggested that plants are aware of what goes on around them. They seem to pick up a great deal of information by ESP. Backster's plants even reacted to his thoughts about them when he was far away.

Plants seem to react in a positive way, by growing fast and healthily, to people who are kind to them, especially those who think good things about them.

Tests have been carried out to see what encourages plant growth. On the right is a simple experiment you can try to see if your thoughts can affect the way plants grow.

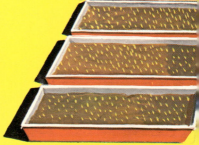

1 Plant three trays of quick-growing seeds, such as cress, and number each one. Remember to use the same quality soil in each seed tray. The 'psychic conditions' for each tray will be different and you can compare the results after a few days.

► Cleve Backster is an expert on polygraphs—lie detectors that work by measuring the electrical resistance of a person's skin. He decided to connect a plant to a polygraph and see what would happen. The results surprised him as the plant produced a pattern of tracings similar to those made by people, almost as if it was experiencing emotions.

Backster decided to burn a leaf. At the very moment he made up his mind, the plant showed a huge reaction on the polygraph. It seemed to have read his mind and understood Backster's intention to hurt it. Plants seem to recognize a killer. A plant that had witnessed the destruction of another plant, showed a frenzied reaction when the person who had killed it entered the same room.

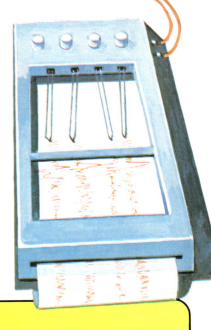

2 Try thinking kind thoughts about tray one. Do not think about tray two at all. Spend a few minutes every day 'hating' the seeds in tray three—imagine they are evil and ungrateful. You must give each tray the same amount of water and sunlight.

3 After talking to, and thinking about, your cress plants for a few days, you may notice a difference between the way each tray of seeds has grown. You can do many kinds of tests like this and perhaps find the best way to grow your plants.

Psychic medicine

Medicine in industrially developed countries relies mostly on well-trained doctors, giving patients expensive drugs and performing difficult surgical operations. In other parts of the world, psychics, 'witch-doctors' and holy men of different religious faiths have been curing people in amazing and unexplainable ways for thousands of years.

Many people appear to have the power to use 'psychic medicine'. This is the general term for ways of curing people that involves psychic powers.

The sleeping doctor

Edgar Cayce was born in Kentucky USA, in 1877. In his early 20s he lost his voice after an attack of laryngitis. Years of medical treatment did not help, so in utter desperation he went to a hypnotist, seeking a cure. Once put into a deep trance, Cayce began to speak in a clear strong voice. He described what was wrong with his throat and how it should be cured. The remedy worked and Cayce decided to see if he could help other people in the same way.

In the 43 years before his death in 1945, Cayce dealt with over 30,000 people with many different diseases, always diagnosing and treating them while in a hypnotic trance. This strange ability earned him the nickname 'the sleeping doctor'.

Psychic surgeon

In 1950 a Brazilian, known as Arigo, claimed that he had been taken over by the spirit of 'Dr Fritz', a German surgeon who died in World War I. Arigo said that one night the doctor appeared and told him that he was going to cure the sick through him. Arigo soon began going into trances and performing medical operations with ordinary scissors and knives.

Witnesses said he looked stunned and spoke with a German accent. Afterwards he could not remember doing the surgery. Yet he had cut people open with a kitchen knife, thrust his hands inside their bodies to remove diseased parts and closed the

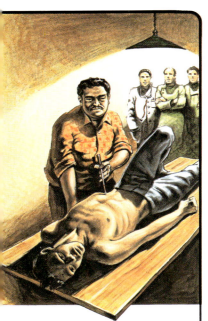

wounds by pressing the edges together. His patients seemed to feel no pain.

Doctors who have seen Arigo and other psychic surgeons at work are quite baffled. Some people think that the operations of the psychic surgeons are merely conjuring tricks. Despite these doubts, many patients have recovered from otherwise incurable diseases.

Most psychic surgeons claim they are guided by the spirits of doctors who have died but who wish to carry on helping the sick. They say that, because they are using supernatural powers, they are not bound by natural laws and that is why their patients feel no pain and recover so quickly and easily.

Healing hands

In the most common method of psychic healing, the healer simply puts his hands on the patient's body. Many healers say that they can feel a kind of energy leave their bodies when they work. The patients often feel a tingling sensation where the healer's hand touches them.

Many healers believe the healing power comes from God and they are only a medium, through which God's power passes.

One Hungarian healer, named Estebany, has been tested by scientists. A group of mice had small cuts made in their skin. Some had no treatment, some were held by Estebany for twenty minutes, twice a day and others were held by students for an equal length of time. Those held by Estebany recovered much faster than the others.

Estebany was also able to increase the rate at which plants grew. The plants were given water to drink that had previously been held in the healer's hands.

Dowsing

Dowsing or 'divining' is a simple and, apparently often successful method of finding something that is hidden.

The earliest recorded dowsers were 16th century German miners. They used forked twigs of hazelwood to search for copper, tin and lead in the area of the Harz Mountains. People have dowsed for many different substances apart from precious metal. One of the most common uses of dowsing has been water divining—searching for sources of water.

How dowsing works is a mystery. It involves no physical contact with the object being sought, or with the surroundings of the object. Some people think that divining rods might register small changes in the Earth's magnetic field.

Although dowsing is still not completely understood, it is widely used in industries such as building and mining, which need to locate underground pipes and sources of water or minerals. Perhaps dowsing will become an accepted scientific technique.

Make your own dowsing rods

Researchers in the USA in 1977 found that 99% of the people they tested could get a reaction of some kind, when using divining rods.

If you would like to test your own skill as a dowser, you can make your own equipment very simply and cheaply from the instructions given here.

50cm
BEND HERE
10cm
40cm

▲ You need two strips of fairly stiff wire, each about 50cm long and 2mm thick. Metal coat hangers, straightened and cut to length with pliers, are ideal for making dowsing rods. Bend each strip of wire into an 'L' shape so that one side is 10cm long and the other is 40cm long. These will form your dowsing or divining rods.

170

How to dowse

Many different tools can be used for dowsing, though traditionally a forked twig from a hazel tree is thought to be the most sensitive to the mysterious force involved.

The dowser holds the twig lightly in his hands and walks over an area where he thinks there might be something hidden. It could be water, gold, oil or anything at all that the dowser wishes to search for. While walking, he must concentrate his mind on the object of his search and think hard about it.

When he is immediately above what he is looking for, the twig should dip down suddenly.

First ask someone to place ten identical pieces of paper on the floor and to hide a coin under one of them. Hold the rods with their long arms parallel to the floor, pointing out in front of you. Now begin to walk around the room, over each book, thinking hard about the coin. The rods should swing together and cross over as you pass over the sheet of paper which is hiding the coin.

GLUE HERE

▲ To make a holder for the rods you need two hollow tubes of stiff cardboard, each about 10cm long with a diameter of one cm. The holders could be made out of four empty cotton reels instead. Glue two cotton reels together to make each holder.

Now place the short side of the wire strips into the centre of the holders.

171

Dowsing and tracking

As well as finding small objects, dowsers can track the course of underground cables or drain pipes.

The two ways used to trace the course of an underground pipe are shown below.

The first method is to walk backwards and forwards over the area where the pipe may be hidden, while thinking of the pipe. Note each place where the forked twig reacts— the pipe should lie in a line beneath those points.

The second method is to 'ask' the divining rods to follow the course of the pipe. When they are parallel to each other you should be above the pipe.

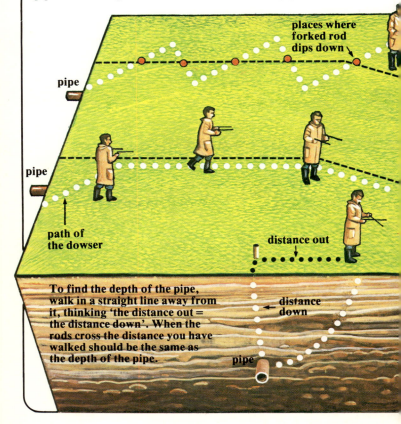

places where forked rod dips down

pipe

pipe

path of the dowser

distance out

To find the depth of the pipe, walk in a straight line away from it, thinking 'the distance out = the distance down'. When the rods cross the distance you have walked should be the same as the depth of the pipe.

distance down

pipe

Dowsing with maps

Some people can dowse from a distance, using a map of the area where they think something may be hidden.

Like ordinary dowsing, you can try looking for anything you can fix in your mind's eye. As you look at a map, imagine that you are walking over the area.

Robert Leftwich, an English dowser and clairvoyant pictured here, can find old tunnels and sources of water using a map, a pendulum and a pointer to direct his concentration.

Perhaps some dowsing depends on the abilities of the dowser. There may be no mysterious force connecting the things a dowser finds with the tools used to find them. Two ways of dowsing with a map and a pendulum are described below.

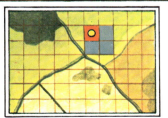

▲ Ask 'Is the object here?' of a large area on the map. Gradually limit the size of the area questioned until it is narrowed down to a single point on the map.

▲ Ask 'Which way is the object?' Follow the direction in which the pendulum swings until, when you are pointing to the object, it should start to rotate in a circle.

Testing ESP

It is only in the last century that ESP—telepathy, clairvoyance and precognition—have been scientifically studied. Scientists demand that an experiment must be able to be repeated with similar results before they will accept it as evidence. It could be just a coincidence that someone knows what another person is thinking, or that someone can guess what is going to happen in the future. In order to check whether psychic powers are real and not just coincidences, tests are designed to be simple and repeatable.

ESP does not always work just because people want it to. They often feel that the unfamiliar setting of a scientific laboratory can hinder their psychic powers. Experiments where the tester and subject are optimistic about the results seem to be the most successful.

Dr J B Rhine, an American researcher who coined the term 'ESP' in the 1930s, set out to test if psychic powers were real. He used a pack of specially designed cards, called Zener cards, shown above. Each card has one of five simple and easily recognized patterns on it. Dr Rhine wanted to see if people could guess which card was being picked from the pack. There are five cards of each pattern in the pack. Because of this, it was expected that, on average, people would make five correct guesses out of 25.

Rhine found, however, that some people consistently got much higher scores. One person even guessed correctly all 25 cards. The odds against this happening by chance alone, without some sort of ESP, are astronomical. A few people could guess a card even before it had been picked out of the pack. Similar tests have been carried out all over the world and most seem to show that psychic powers cannot be dimissed as the results of pure coincidence.

Test your own telepathy

Telepathy, clairvoyance and precognition are the easiest ESP powers to test. You can buy or make Zener cards for the experiments. You should also make score charts, like the one on the right for the subject to mark his guesses on. You need one chart for each test with the pack of 25 cards. Divide the chart into five columns (one for each symbol) and then draw 25 lines across the columns, so you have line 1 for the first guess and so on. The subject puts one tick on each line, under the symbol which he thinks is on the card that the tester has picked. Remember to shuffle the cards well, before each test, to make sure they are in a random order.

When testing for telepathy the subject should not be able to see the tester, who must call 'now' when picking each card. The tester looks at it and tries to 'beam' the symbol to the subject's mind.

Clairvoyance can be tested

by one person. Hold the pack of cards face down and try to guess which symbol is on the other side as you choose each card. Do not turn them over until the end of the test.

Sometimes a person can guess a card correctly before it is picked. Check to see if a guess is correct for the card which follows. This could be evidence of precognition.

In all three tests, scores of five out of 25 are expected by chance alone, but higher scores could be due to ESP.

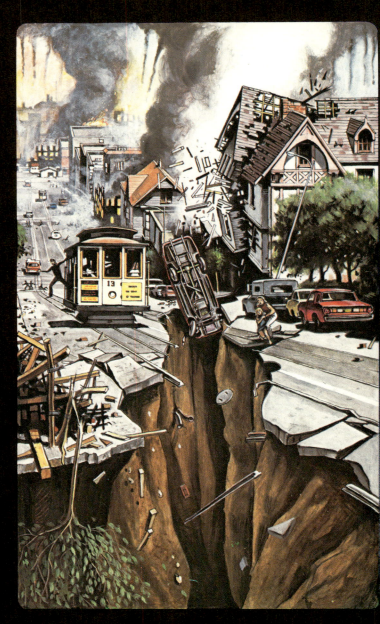

Using ESP

Extra-sensory perception and strange forces of all kinds may be known to exist, but we still understand very little about them. Even so, these mysterious powers could be made to work for us.

Saving San Francisco

On April 6 1906, the city of San Francisco, on the west coast of the USA was partly destroyed by an earthquake. A quarter of a million people were made homeless and about 700 were killed. Many people think the city will be hit by another earthquake in the future, but predicting exactly when this will come is not an easy job for scientists.

Research into premonitions has shown that extra-sensory perception may be able to help give the people of San Francisco an early warning of disaster. Quite often when a major disaster occurs, people start having premonitions some weeks, or even months, before the tragedy happens.

In 1966, a coal tip slid onto a school in Wales, killing nearly 150 people. Many dreamed about the accident before it happened. Studies of the precognitive dreams that were reported showed that there were more and more of these premonitions as the time of the disaster approached.

Researchers in California have now started to collect all the reports of dreams about the expected earthquake. They think the number of premonitions about the disaster will increase as the time for the earthquake grows near. They will then be able to warn the people of San Francisco that their earthquake is coming.

Thought-controlled world?

ESP and psychokinesis may one day be used to control machines. An American inventor has found a way of using his thought power to switch on the engine of his car. First he directed his thoughts to plants that were wired up to a lie detector. When the plants received his 'message', their reactions were made to send out a radio signal which operated the car's ignition. One radio signal, however, could have been sent straight to the car without the use of telepathy.

The governments of the USA and the USSR are both looking for ways to use ESP in their weapons of war and means of defence. One Russian experiment was aimed at using telepathic brain signals to pass messages to their fleet of submarines.

They took some baby rabbits down in a submarine and kept their mother on land. Radio waves cannot pass through deep water, but the Russians found that the brain waves of rabbits can. They killed the baby rabbits one by one and measured the mother's brain activity. At each death there was a definite reaction that could have been made to trigger an electrical switch.

Weird world

Many of the strange events we have looked at so far in this book have occurred because some people seem to possess mysterious psychic powers. However, there are other, possibly stranger things, happening all over the world, which might never be satisfactorily explained.

There are stories of strange monsters, UFOs, stones that move, statues coming to life and many other weird things. It seems impossible to prove whether or not these things do occur, yet they are seen or experienced so often, by so many people, that it is also impossible to dismiss them.

▲ In 1938 a Japanese man put his dead sister's favourite doll in a temple. Returning to collect it nine years later, he saw that its hair had grown. The doll's hair is still growing and it is said the little girl's spirit is living through the doll.

▲ In Britain when it rains hard, people say it is raining 'cats and dogs', yet sometimes strange things do fall from the skies. Falls of fishes and frogs have been seen, black rain, showers of blood and even money. Many of these have natural, if rather odd, explanations. Freak winds can carry small objects up into the air and deposit them some distance away. However, some falls cannot be explained. In 1503 a shower of wooden crosses was reported to have fallen from the skies.

▲ Many parts of the world have been haunted by mysterious hoof and footprints. In 1855 a trail of hoof prints which went right over roofs and walls appeared overnight in Dorset. They looked like the tracks of a two legged, hoofed animal.

▲ There have been many stories of statues and pictures which mysteriously bleed or weep. They are usually religious images, often those of Christ and the Virgin Mary. Some have been scientifically analyzed and the blood or tears found to be real.

▲ It is rumoured that both American and Russian scientists have experimented with trying to make things invisible. One story tells of a US Navy ship, moored in Philadelphia harbour in the 1940s. It began to glow green, then suddenly vanished. At the same moment it was seen about 350km away in Norfolk harbour and was later spotted at sea appearing and disappearing. All information was kept top secret — but some say the US Navy was experimenting with strong electro-magnetic generators.

179

Stones of mystery

In most European countries, there are circles and lines of gigantic standing stones that were built by the peoples who lived over 5,000 years ago. No-one really knows how these prehistoric monuments were built or what they were used for. Some are merely huge single stones which perch on the top of a hill.

Many of the circles are said to have been astronomical observatories. The stones were probably also sites of worship and even sacrifice. Dowsers report finding strong forces, powerful enough to cause dizziness or even illness in these ancient places.

Ley lines

In 1921 Alfred Watkins first suggested that many prehistoric sites were built along straight lines. He called them 'ley lines' and thought they were paths or routes used by ancient man when travelling. Watkins felt the leys followed natural landmarks, like hills, and thought the stones were man-made 'sign posts'.

Today there is a theory that the leys are lines of natural power that comes from the Earth. Some people claim that prehistoric man was aware of, and worshipped this force and put up the stones in places along the ley line where it felt strongest.

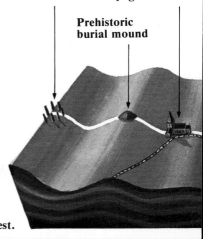

Circle of stones

Prehistoric burial mound

Churches often built on older pagan sites

▲ Bill Lewis, a British dowser, felt a strong force seeping out of the ground and going up one standing stone in a spiral. When it was tested, scientists found the stone had bands of magnetic power going round it, in about the places Lewis had indicated.

Single standing stone

Deep notches cut in skyline

Ancient river crossing

Springs or 'Holy' wells

▲ Ancient stones are often surrounded by folklore and legend. Stones with holes in the middle were said to have the power to heal sick people, if they were passed through the hole. This practice went on in parts of Britain until the end of the 19th century.

Pyramid power

The Great Pyramid of Cheops was built at Giza in Egypt on the west bank of the Nile in about 3000BC. It took thousands of men over 30 years to build, and it still stands today as an awe-inspiring monument to the Pharaoh Cheops. The Great Pyramid seems to possess some very mysterious powers.

A Frenchman named Bovis, was once looking round the King's Chamber, where the body of the Pharaoh was laid. He found that some animals that had wandered into the chamber and died there, had dried out and become preserved like mummies. He built a model pyramid and put a dead cat inside in it to test its power. The cat's corpse did not rot.

In 1959 a Czech engineer found that if a blunt razor blade was placed on a stand in the centre of a model of the Great Pyramid, it became sharp again. One theory is that the shape of the pyramid acts as a focus for some sort of unknown force which can preserve or restore objects.

It is easy to test whether the pyramid's shape does have any special properties by making a simple cardboard model. The model must be left on a north-south line, like the real pyramid at Giza. Instead of a razor, you can test fresh food, such as butter. Place it on the stand in the centre. This represents the height of the pharaoh's burial chamber.

Test your own pyramid

With the pattern below, you can make an accurate scale model of the Great Pyramid at Giza. You can test its powers for yourself.

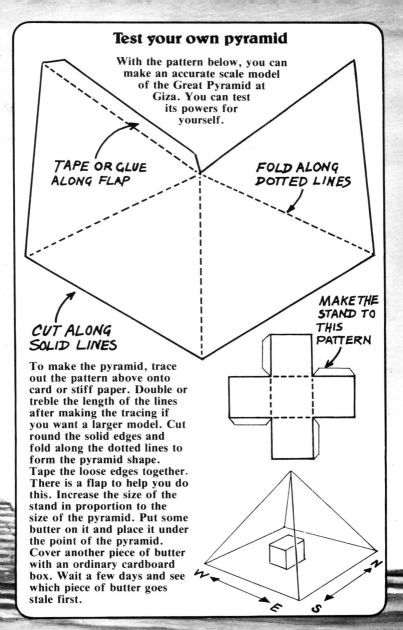

TAPE OR GLUE ALONG FLAP

FOLD ALONG DOTTED LINES

CUT ALONG SOLID LINES

MAKE THE STAND TO THIS PATTERN

To make the pyramid, trace out the pattern above onto card or stiff paper. Double or treble the length of the lines after making the tracing if you want a larger model. Cut round the solid edges and fold along the dotted lines to form the pyramid shape. Tape the loose edges together. There is a flap to help you do this. Increase the size of the stand in proportion to the size of the pyramid. Put some butter on it and place it under the point of the pyramid. Cover another piece of butter with an ordinary cardboard box. Wait a few days and see which piece of butter goes stale first.

W E S N

The Bermuda triangle

Since 1945, over a hundred ships and planes and more than a thousand people have disappeared in an area of sea known as the 'Bermuda Triangle'.

Even in the days of sailing ships, it was rumoured to be a dangerous place. Sea monsters were said to attack the ships and eat the sailors. They were blamed for vessels which were found drifting aimlessly without any crew on board.

In the past, the Bermudas were known as 'The Isles of the Devils', and it was said that demons caused all the strange disappearances.

▲ The triangle runs from the tip of Florida to Puerto Rico and on to Bermuda. It is one of the few places in the world where the compass points to true north and this leads some people to think that a strange electro-magnetic force is to blame.

▲ Christopher Columbus was the first European to sail through the triangle. He reported that the sea was lit by a weird glow and a huge ball of fire shot out of the ocean. The ship's compass was disturbed by an unexplained magnetic force.

▲ In 1964, a pilot flying over the triangle found that he could not control his plane as all the electrical instruments were behaving erratically. For a period of ten minutes, the whole plane glowed with a pale green phosphorescent light.

The vanishing patrol

On the afternoon of
December 5th, 1945, a whole
patrol of American naval
aircraft went missing over the
Bermuda Triangle. The five
planes and 14 man crew of
Flight 19, took off from Fort
Lauderdale in Florida, at
about two o'clock. The
weather was fine and all the
crew were experienced fliers.
It was just a routine training
mission, yet one man dropped
out at the last moment
because he had a premonition
of disaster.

At about 3.15 p.m. the
Fort Lauderdale control
tower received an unexpected
message from Flight 19—it
was lost. The flight leader

radioed in, reporting that they
had lost their bearings and
gone off course. The
instruments did not seem to
be working, so they could not
tell which way was west. The
pilot said that everything,
even the ocean, looked
strange and they could not
see land. After 15 minutes,
radio contact was lost.

A rescue craft was sent out
straight away. Control tower
received only one message
from this plane, before it too
vanished. Nothing was found
of the six planes, even after
weeks of searching.

An enquiry was held but
the investigators said they
could not even make a guess
as to what happened on that
fateful December afternoon.

Unidentified flying objects

Some people believe that many mysteries can be explained by interference from alien beings from outer space. One theory even suggests that such creatures may have helped build ancient pyramids and stone circles.

UFO's have also been blamed for strange disappearances of boats and aircraft in areas like the Bermuda Triangle. It is supposed the aliens collect specimens of human life and technology to study.

In 1915 a whole regiment of the British Army walked up to the top of a cloud covered hill in Turkey and completely vanished. They were never heard of again and some people think the soldiers may have been captured by a UFO.

In the past 30 years, many people have claimed they have been kidnapped for a time by aliens in flying saucers. Uri Geller is even reported to have said that his mysterious powers are a gift from an alien civilization.

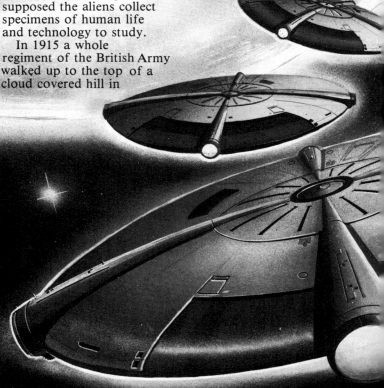

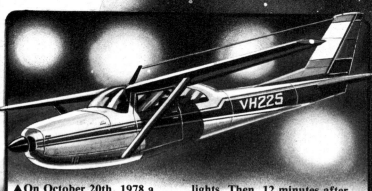

▲On October 20th, 1978 a young pilot flying a short distance from King Island, Australia, radioed the base at Melbourne that a strange unidentifiable craft was hovering around his plane. He described it as a long, fast moving object with four lights. Then, 12 minutes after his first report, the pilot and his plane vanished, but his UFO sighting was later confirmed by witnesses on the mainland.

Sightings of cigar-shaped UFOs have been reported in the area on and off since 1896.

The "hollow" earth

▲Weather satellite pictures of Earth sometimes show shadows around the poles. They have been used to support the unlikely theory that UFO's are sent out from deep inside our 'hollow' Earth —through holes in the North and South poles.

Mysterious powers quiz

Now that you have read all about mysterious powers and strange forces, test your knowledge by trying to answer these questions. The answers are at the bottom of the next page. They are printed upside down and back to front to make cheating more difficult. In order to read them, hold the page upside down in front of a mirror.

1 Which 19th century medium once levitated in and out of a top floor window?

2 What is the most common sort of ESP experience?

3 Who first tested plants with a lie detector?

4 What is said to connect the astral body to the physical body during astral travel?

5 Which English prophetess foresaw the fire of London?

6 Who was one of the earliest sailors to report mysterious happenings in what is now called the Bermuda Triangle?

7 What did President Abraham Lincoln foresee in a dream?

8 What is the name given to fortune telling with cards?

9 What power were standing stones with holes in the middle said to possess?

10 What word are the letters 'PK' short for?

11 Which poet was warned of his death by drowning by the visit of his own double?

12 What ESP powers are tested with Zener cards?

13 What effect do models of the Cheops pyramid seem to have on blunt razor blades?

14 How many Catholic saints were said to have levitated?

15 Who claims to be able to take 'thought photographs' by staring into a camera?

16 What ESP ability is used to locate underground sources of water and minerals?

17 Who were the earliest recorded dowsers?

18 What sort of cards are the best for fortune telling?

19 Which hypnotist is said to have helped people remember their 'past lives'?

20 What effect did Estebany seem to have on injured mice in an experiment?

21 What are crystal balls sometimes used for?

22 What happens to electrical equipment on board ships and planes while they are in the Bermuda Triangle?

23 Where is there a doll whose hair is growing?

24 Where did soldiers witness visions of angels and saints during World War One?

25 Which planet did Ingo Swann visit in a 'remote viewing' experiment in 1974?

26 Where did the soldier who was teleported to Mexico City in 1593, come from?

27 Who first developed the theory of ley-lines?

28 What was the name of the 17th century Italian monk who levitated while praying?

29 What sort of music seems to encourage plants to grow faster and stronger?

30 What is the name given to the process which apparently photographs the electrical auras of living things?

31 What is seeing your own double said to foretell?

32 What paranormal power is Uri Geller most famous for?

33 In which American city is there a bureau to monitor premonitions of disaster?

34 How many people reported having premonitions about the Titanic sinking?

35 What is the term 'OOBE' short for?

36 Which Catholic nun was said to have teleported herself to America over 500 times?

37 What do some doctors and dentists use hypnotism for?

38 What do some people believe might be responsible for the strange disappearances in the Bermuda Triangle?

39 What did the seers of Ancient Egypt gaze into, to encourage their visions of the future?

40 Which American researcher coined the phrase 'ESP'?

Answers

1   Daniel Home.
2   Precognitive dreams.
3   Cleve Backster.
4   A luminous silver cord.
5   Mother Shipton.
6   Christopher Columbus.
7   People mourning his death.
8   Cartomancy.
9   Healing powers.
10 Psychokinesis.
11 Shelley.
12 Precognition, telepathy and clairvoyance.
13 A sharpening effect.
14 More than 200.
15 Ted Serios.
16 Dowsing.
17 16th century German miners.
18 Tarot cards.
19 Astral projection.
20 A healing influence.
21 Fortune telling.
22 It sometimes stops working.
23 A Japanese temple.
24 Nora and Apres.
25 Mercury.
26 The Philippines.
27 Astral walking.
28 St Joseph of Copertino.
29 Kind thoughts.
30 Kirlian photography.
31 Impending doom, especially death.
32 Bending metal forks and spoons by stroking them.
33 San Francisco.
34 More than 20.
35 Out-of-the-body experience.
36 Sister Mary of Agreda.
37 Preventing their patients feeling pain.
38 UFO's.
39 Pools of blood.
40 Dr J B Rhine.

Index